THE MAYOR
OF
FOLSOM STREET

The Auto/Biography
of
"Daddy Alan" Selby
aka Mr. S

THE MAYOR OF FOLSOM STREET

The Auto/Biography of "Daddy Alan" Selby aka Mr. S

by Jordy Jones

Fair Page Media LLC
Springfield, PA

Photographs © David Rhodes of *The Leather Journal*: used by permission

Front cover design by Thom Magister

ISBN: 978-0-9989098-0-6

This project is dedicated, of course, to Daddy Alan Selby.

If he were alive, I think he would dedicate it to his boys
Peter Jacklin and Johnie Garcia and his beloved favorite charity, *AEF*.

If he were alive, I expect he would write pages of dedications.
It was the way he was, you see.

If he were alive, I know he would dedicate his story to the
community.

On the occasion of the founding of the *Leather Archive and Museum Selby Fund*, he wrote:

I would like to thank everyone in the entire leather community for
your support and friendship over the years. You are my family; I love
and appreciate you all more than words can fully convey.

Contents

ACKNOWLEDGMENTS

Thanks to all those who have encouraged me in bringing his story to this stage. I would like to particularly acknowledge the following individuals and organizations for their support, both material and personal, of this project:

Victoria Baker, Race Bannon, Joseph Bean, Robert Davolt, Joshua Aidan Dunn, Peter Fiske, Jack Fritscher, Steve Gaynes, Mark Hemry, Dorian Katz, Tony Koester, Robert Lawrence, Joel Manon, Virgil Petrie, Carol Queen, Robert Roberts, Gayle Rubin, Sally Stein, Willie Walker, and my beloved husband, Marty Tackitt-Jones.

A special thanks to Dave Rhodes of *The Leather Journal* for providing the photographs included in the book and to Thom Magister for designing the front cover.

Organizations to which I am grateful include *The Center for Sex and Culture, The GLBT Historical Society / History Museum, Cleveland Leather Alliance Weekend, The Leather Archives and Museum, San Francisco State University, Southern Illinois University at Carbondale* and *The University of California at Irvine.*

PART I: THE INTRODUCTION

INTRODUCTION

"Kinky is British for weird."[1]

Daddy Alan. Who was he? He was a man of his time, a 20th century man. He was a man of many places, a traveller, an expatriate, and an immigrant: an Englishman who ultimately became an American. He was a gentleman, a leatherman, a rubberman, and a veteran of the Royal Navy. He was creative and passionate, a hard worker and a harder player, and he was very, very kinky. He was a good salesman and a mediocre businessman. He was a people person. He was a legend. He was a peach of a man with a plum of a voice. Alan Selby: The "S" in Mr. S Leather; the original San Francisco Leather Daddy; the Mayor of Folsom Street.[2]

This is the introduction to his story, and words about him. They are my words, and the words of others who knew him. It is a hybrid text. It includes original material that he never mentioned in his interviews and notes, and alternate viewpoints on his favorite tales. It includes multiple voices. For something close to his own words, skip the introduction and go on to the "auto" part of the auto/biography. Then come back here if you want. Or start at the index; it is a document of its own. A quick look will reveal the scope of his influence -so many places, events, and people -a network that only becomes clear with time and distance. Perverts, punks, and philosophers: he dressed and

---

[1] Paul Newman in *Harper*, directed by Jack Smight (1966; Warner Bros.)

[2] Mary Richards, *Bay Area Reporter*, October 13, 1988.

undressed them all; he held many when they were laughing, crying, and even dying.

He had a sense of his own place in history and wanted to write it. He did write some of it. But he was always busy with other things, mostly taking care of people. He died before he was able to finish and publish. He took notes and he had help along the way. Fellow Englishman David Normand-Harris interviewed him in 1999. Those transcripts, together with his own notes, form the base of his story as he wanted it told. His auto/biography is a post-mortem literary collaboration. The late Robert Davolt worked on it. Joseph Bean, alive and well and retired to Maui, worked on it. When Alan passed, his "archive" passed to me. Jacques Derrida said: "the archive has always been a pledge, and like every pledge, a token of the future."[3]

Archive may be a misleading word for what Alan left behind. Alan needed to be needed, and was always busy helping others. As a result of this, he sometimes neglected his own infrastructure. Papers, pins, photographs, souvenirs, letters, important historical objects and ten-year-old receipts would all be pushed into drawers to be gone through later. In Alan's universe, people were more important than things, and later never came. His walls were crowded with the awards he had received over the years, and his closet was brimming with his wardrobe. People gave him little presents, and stuffed animals, and he kept them. He was sentimental that way. I helped him keep surfaces clear and the most important items accessible. For the last two years of his life, he had a roommate, Tony Koester, who was also San Francisco Leather Daddy XX. Koester had a boy, Christopher Smith, who moved in, and the three of them enjoyed a supportive, loving and crowded, home life. Smith died tragically not long before Alan, and his possessions were still in the apartment when Alan passed. When Alan died, Koester initially thought he might keep the place, and continued living there. But auras of the departed sometimes cling to things and it was not long before he was tired of living with ghosts. It was time to move and that meant it was time to pack. Koester packed his things

---

[3] Jacques Derrida, *Archive Fever,* (Chicago: University of Chicago, 1995), 18.

and his boy's things in the room that had been theirs. I packed Alan's things in his room, and we met occasionally in the hallway to hold one another and cry. We sorted and distributed for a week. Some things went to friends. His leather went to The Leather Archives and Museum in Chicago. The rest I put into boxes and took with me to Southern California, where I was going to graduate school at the University of California at Irvine. I did nothing with it for several years. I was busy reading, writing, being examined, defending, and teaching. I missed him, and little by little, began to go through the archive. Eventually, I realized that if his story were going to be told, I would have to be the one to tell it. His story was there in those boxes, in his "archive."

In *The History of Sexuality*, the famous French philosopher (and homosexual pervert) Michel Foucault linked normal/ized sexualities and political repression. He combed archives to tell a tale of how sex came to mean what it did and function as it did. The taxonomic frenzy of the nineteenth century categorized everything. What Charles Darwin did with living organisms, Sigmund Freud did with the human psyche. Everything needed a name and a proper function. The emerging social sciences, including the nascent discipline of sexology, used the concept of speciation as a strategy to "ensure population, to reproduce labor capacity (and) to constitute a sexuality that is economically useful and politically conservative."[4] With the one and only *right* way plotted, all other libidinal avenues become suspect and subject to scrutiny and regulation. Dad works and dominates. Mom supports him and is submissive. Children are obedient and sexually innocent. And society is safe. But there is always a flipside to history. It took an archive-crawling pervert to pull it out and break it down. The historic sodomite who did something bad morphed into the modern homosexual, who *was* something bad. Beyond the sodomite, Foucault found the homosexual and "underneath the libertine, the pervert."[5] He identified a succession

---

[4] Michel Foucault, *The History of Sexuality, vol. 1: An Introduction* (New York: Random House, 1978), 37.

[5] Ibid., 40.

of "peripheral sexualities" whose sheer volume suggests a potentially infinite proliferation:

> To marry a close relative or practice sodomy, to seduce a nun or engage in sadism, to deceive one's wife or violate cadavers, became things that were essentially different...children wise beyond their years, precocious little girls, ambiguous schoolboys, dubious servants and educators, cruel and maniacal husbands, solitary collectors, ramblers with bizarre impulses. This was the numberless family of perverts who were on friendly terms with delinquents and akin to madmen.[6]

Foucault identified perversion, and was identified as a pervert. According to leather[7] historian Jack Fritscher: "...in the 1980s, it fell to that freaky visitor to Folsom Street, the irrepressible French philosopher Foucault "The S&M Poster Boy," to probe the human psyche far deeper. Foucault twisted S&M leather recreational sex into existential endgame."[8]

It was also in the 1980s, in San Francisco's South of Market (SOMA) neighborhood, that the Frenchman Michel Foucault made the acquaintance of the Englishman Alan Selby. It was in this context that Alan sometimes mentioned "that nice French boy, Michel."[9] He met him. He knew him casually. He probed him very deeply. But he was no star-fucker. He was a fellow soldier in the war against the oppression

---

[6] Ibid., 39-40.

[7] "Leather" is a multi-faceted and ambiguous tem, which is variously used to refer to the material, the sexual style, and the subculture. It is used in all these forms in here. Jack Fritscher has called leather "a code word for dominance and submission in the human condition." Jack Fritscher, "Introduction: Leather, *Dolce Vita*, Pop Culture, and the Prime of Mr. Larry Townsend," Larry Townsend, *Leathermen's Handbook Silver Anniversary Edition*, (Los Angeles: L.T. Publications, 1997), 9.

[8] Ibid., 11.

[9] Alan Selby, Personal communication, circa 2002.

of sexual minorities, and he was horny. He knew the nice boy Michel, but he had no idea who "Foucault" was.

Many years later, I met Alan Selby. Alan liked to fuck and he liked to fist. He liked to tie boys up and he liked to take control. He took the Frenchman and he took me. He took so many and he gave so much back to so many more. He had a phoenix tattooed on his right arm and a dragon on his left. These were courtesy of Mr. Sebastian of London. The phoenix' beak pointed to his wrist, while the fiery tail feathers ran up towards his elbow. He would joke about using it as a depth gauge: "When the tail feathers disappear...well!" This was a man who could reach into a boy and hold his beating heart in his hand.

More dominant and kinky than strictly sadistic, Alan was a notorious flirt who mentored hundreds and fucked thousands. Those he knew became better, stronger, more knowledgeable and more powerful for having known him. He led through example, not self-promotion or coercion. He was an inspiration. "Daddy" Alan Selby was an important figure in the history of leather, and one from whom future generations can glean valuable lessons about the importance of good humor, fearlessness, service to others, and working every bit as hard as we play.

Alan Selby was born Alan Henry Sniders in Yorkshire, England on the 12th of February, 1929. He survived the British public school system, which we in the United States call private or preparatory education. He was awarded the School Certificate of the Oxford and Cambridge Schools Examination Board in December of 1945. British boys' boarding schools have long provided a backdrop for sadomasochistic (S/m) fantasies and scenarios. The discipline, the hierarchy, the sodomy, the canings! Even the terminology is evocative. Headmasters, houses, prefects, and of course, the notorious "head boy." Whatever peculiar predilections we may bring with us into the world, our early experiences refine our later trajectories, as perverts or as anything else. It was no different with the young Alan.

Alan had an older brother, whom he would never describe in later years as anything but "my despicable brother." Why? An unstated rule of family life, whether it is biological, chosen or leather family, is that the more powerful members ought to protect the more vulnerable. When this contract is broken, trust goes with it. Alan called his brother "my *despicable* brother." What earned such lifelong contempt? Those who knew Alan knew how very rare it was for him to speak ill of anyone. "I don't much care for that man," said about those very few who regularly spoke ill of him, was about as harsh as it ever got. He was a gentleman, through and through. Those who knew him well also knew of his lifelong dislike of cigars. A bit of old school history answers the leather history trivia question: "Why did Alan Selby hate cigars so much?" It also provides insight into the man he would become.

When Alan started public school in the late 1930s, at about age eleven, his brother, several years older, was already a prefect – a young man of authority on his way to being head boy. He led the gang of bullies who ran their house, and they terrorized the younger students who were their charges. That is a tradition, and one that Alan's brother really enjoyed. It is also a tradition for older brothers to protect their younger siblings, but that was one he didn't care for so much. Instead of protecting his kid brother, he organized "playful" assaults in which he and his cronies would pin Alan to the ground in the common room and force-feed him cigar smoke. He gagged, they laughed, and he remembered.

Social subjects – and we are all social subjects – are formed, at least in part, through being named. We are called out: "Hey, You!"[10] as Louis Althusser put it. You nerd, you sissy, you nigger, you spic, you bitch, you faggot, you fill-in-the-blank. X marks the social stain. Or, as Pee-wee Herman would reply: "I know you are, but what am I?"[11] There is always "something wrong" with the victim. Alan's brother was a bully and Alan was his victim. A boy becomes a bully through the

---

[10] Louis Althusser, "Ideology and Ideological State Apparatuses," *Lenin and Philosophy and other Essays* (New York, Monthly Review Press, 1971).

[11] Paul Reubens in *Pee-wee's Big Adventure*, directed by Tim Burton (1985; Warner Bros)

act of bullying. He ceases to be a bully only when he ceases to bully. The bully is not a rebel or an outlaw as much as he might like to think he is. He does not subvert the social hierarchy but rather enforces it. Generally he protects up and attacks down. He takes lunch money. He picks on the little kids. He chirps "faggot" in the hallways. He tightens the noose at the lynching, and then enjoys a good picnic. Often, he's a good boy at home, at church, even with school administrators. Alan swore to himself that he himself would *never* be a victim again, and - even more importantly - swore that he would *never, ever* be a bully, and he never was. Instead, he became "Daddy" Alan, the benevolent and "very kinky" protector and champion. And what of his despicable brother? Alan cut him off shortly after school and they never spoke again. But to the end of his life, he really hated the smell of cigars.

Alan did not speak much or often about his early years. But his good friend, the legendary leatherman, whip collector, and Anglophile Peter Fiske, whose recollections were transcribed while Alan was still alive, recalls:

> I've spoken to Alan's English friends, who've known him in some cases for forty years or more. As a matter of fact I even have one friend who went to school with him, and he says that Alan was a live wire even in grammar school. He was always very special and stood out with his incredible energy. Alan tends to keep his friends. He very rarely will break a bond of friendship with someone, and I really have not known him to do it. So people who know him continue to know him, and people who care about him continue to care about him, and he for them.[12]

He enlisted in the Royal Navy at the age of eighteen and served his country as a medic and nurse in the years following World War II. He didn't discuss the war in his interviews with Normand-Harris, but it provided the backdrop of his adolescence and affected his developing psyche. Although never particularly observant, he was one

---

[12] Peter Fiske, Unpublished manuscript, 2001.

of the Tribe. He was a young Jewish Englishman growing up at a time when his country and its allies were deep in a battle with international fascism. That the Germans were using his people as an alibi for their nationalistic ambitions just made the situation more poignant for him. He didn't like bullies in school, not even if their ringleader was his own brother. And he didn't like bullies on the international stage, particularly when they bent his people's history to justify genocide. Many years later, during the peak of the plague years, he would take that youthful sense of moral outrage toward injustice and point it towards the HIV/ AIDS crisis.

After the war, he became a gentlemen's clothier. He also worked in theater, mostly doing stage management. In 1952, for reasons unknown, he changed his last name from Sniders to Selby. During London's "swinging sixties" he worked as a representative for a textile firm and dreamed of starting his own business. During the 1960s he also became increasingly familiar with the homosexual S/m underground. Men would gather casually in locations that featured public attractions such as orators. Speakers Corner in Hyde Park was a popular gathering place, as was Wimbledon Common. Men in riding boots and breeches would cruise one another in the crowd and then slip off together to play indoors, in private. These men dressed for one another's pleasure, and Alan was in the business of dressing gentlemen. It was in Hyde Park in the late 1950s that Alan first met Felix Jones, who was to become a good friend, and who was his initial contact in the world of leather. Alan didn't know that then, though. He was still just an aggressive vanilla top and would remain so for another decade.

David Normand-Harris was a countryman of Alan's own generation, and cruised many of the same outdoor venues. He recounts how a killing chilled the tone of one of the most popular of these, and ultimately killed the scene:

> I went to Wimbledon quite a number of times before the murder took place, and it was absolutely wild, the sound of whips cracking and people tied to trees and so on. It had to be seen and heard to be believed!

The murder was of a policeman, and the murder was committed by a whole lot of youths from a housing estate. One has to go under a major road, the Kingston Bypass. The policeman had been put on the Common to protect the gay people, as far as I understood, and he was in plain clothes, of course. He was taken for a gay man by the yobs from the housing estate, and he was assaulted and murdered. Of course as soon as the murder took place, gay people stopped going; absolutely stopped going to Wimbledon Common.[13]

1969 was a pivotal year for Alan, as it was for the world. That year, at the age of forty, he made his first trip to the United States. It was also the year he decided to start Mr. S Leather. Although he knew many of the men in London's Hyde Park scene through having outfitted them, he had never, until this time, had an actual S/m or leathersex experience. That changed fast and it changed everything. He recounts being picked up in San Francisco and very respectfully schooled by a bottom boy in a tight black leather jacket and tight blue jeans: a very American boy. The men of Hyde Park looked like masters of the hunt. This boy typified a different look, one drawn from post-WWII American motorcycle culture and popularized by Hollywood via Marlon Brando and his gang. By the end of his weekend with the wild one, Alan was a convert: "I was in another world!"[14]

It was also on the return leg of that life-changing 1969 business trip to the States that he was introduced to the rubber fetish scene in New York City. He found that he liked that, too. The president of The 5 Senses Club asked him if he thought there would be interest in a similar organization in England. Alan returned to London with his sexuality revolutionized and bursting with ideas. He placed a small ad in the *Gay News*, and soon the group that would become The RMC

---

[13] David Normand-Harris, From transcripts of interviews with Alan Selby, 1999.

[14] Selby, Personal communication.

(Rubber Man's Club) was meeting. They are still active nearly half a century later.

He joined The 69 and other clubs. He became active in MSC (Motor Sports Club) and FUKC (Federation of United Kingdom Clubs). In The 69, through his good friend Felix Jones, Alan made the acquaintance of fellow associate Touko Laaksonen, better known as Tom of Finland, and they remained friends until the iconic artist's passing. The ease with which Alan was able to recount his interactions with so many artists, activists and seminal organizations highlights his lifelong role as a liaison and ambassador. He moved between micro-communities and used his sales skills and social ease to become a catalyst for positive change.

David Normand-Harris shared many of Alan's memories of that time and place and asked Alan whether he was "…right in thinking that those clubs in London had a little bit of rivalry." He wondered:

> There were some people who were members in common to two or three of them, but in general terms they didn't really meet all that much. I was a member of some of these at certain times. My impression was that RMC, being a smaller group, was a kind of happier little association, and that because of Felix's influence in The 69, that too had good guidance. It had a limited membership, so there were no squabbles and political ups and downs, but MSC had backbiting, and people resigning, and all that sort of thing at various times.[15]

Alan agreed that there were issues, both within and between the clubs, but emphasized the positive interactions and stressed the overlap. He was an optimist in that way and also reluctant to speak ill of anyone.

---

[15] Normand-Harris, From transcripts of interviews.

These were the days in which he was discovering dimensions to his sexuality that he had never known existed. He soaked up the new knowledge and tried new things. Years later, he was to perform a type of self-psychoanalysis in recalling how he understood his boyhood experiences with his "despicable brother." He related those early non-consensual experiences to his only adult experience as a bottom. That particular scene with a French leatherman was a good scene, but it was not his scene. He recalled that he just wanted to flip that top and so he never bottomed again. For the remainder of his life, he remained an exclusive top.

Back in London, Alan met a Mr. Shanks and his friend Mr. Murphy. They owned a leather manufacturing company called SM International. The three men pooled resources, shared designs and together opened a small factory in London. Mr. S Products was launched. He soon met his "very kinky" lover Peter Jacklin, a skilled designer and craftsman specializing in leather craft. To mark the occasion, Jacklin made a bondage collar, which he subsequently wore. It was Jacklin who designed many of the harnesses, studded belts and CBT (Cock & Ball Torture) toys that have since become classics. Alan said of him: "He was a very talented boy and I am pleased that their popularity is a tribute to his memory!"[16]

During most of the 1970s Alan lived an intercontinental lifestyle. He traveled mostly between London and San Francisco, but business took him to many world-class cities, and local leather communities always welcomed him warmly. Alan was a networker well before the term existed. Whether it was business, social life, or activism, Alan mixed. As social animals, we collaborate by nature, and Alan was a natural. In 1972 he was working with Ron Ernst and Pat O'Brien, the owners of Leather 'n' Things in San Francisco's Castro District. They stocked Mr. S products and a friendship had developed between the men. Sometimes they brainstormed next season's products. It was in just such a brainstorming session that they formalized what was to become known as the hanky code. They had overstocked bandannas

---

[16] Selby, Personal communication.

and wanted a way to move them. Some men were already using certain colors to signal specific interests. The three men added several other colors, wrote down a basic hanky code, and published it. It took off like an eagle.

As business grew, Alan Selby and Peter Jacklin opened their own small factory, then their own retail outlet, in Wandsworth, South London. They called it Leather Unlimited. It quickly became a *de facto* community center, with the seminal tattoo artist Alan Oversby (*Mr. Sebastian*) opening a tattoo and piercing salon in the basement of the building. Peter Fiske recalls those days:

> Alan cut quite a swathe through London in the 1970s with the shop. The community in London in those days was not very organized; everything was done - somewhat like San Francisco in the 1960s - through a couple of clubs and bars, so it was a rather small and interconnected community. And one of the major connection points was Alan's shop. He helped come up with one of the first leather caps, the wonderful black leather motorcycle cap that was so popular in the 1960s and 1970s and that seems to have retained its popularity. Alan's come up with lots of ideas, from the Shower Shot for douching, to different kinds of tit clamps, to just all sorts of things![17]

Alan also made contacts, friends and colleagues in the fashion and performing worlds. He and Jacklin did a booming side-business doing custom work to specifications, providing leather bustier forms for punk couturier Vivienne Westwood, as well as stage outfits for Judas Priest and other rockers. Rock-and-roll, as an institution, was beginning to adapt the look of the leathersex underground to signal a neo-dada, proto-postmodern defiance of existing aesthetic norms. In punk, visual references to sadomasochism became common. It wasn't always only about the look. Among young people of that generation

---

[17] Fiske, Unpublished manuscript.

the punk subculture was a viable alternative path into alternative sexualities. It existed alongside, and sometimes overlapped, leathersex subcultures.

With this shift, the groundwork was laid for the eventual mainstreaming of the leather look and to some extent the lifestyle. Alan was to note in later years that there had been those in the scene who disapproved of what they perceived as his role in the popularization of what had historically signaled underground sexualities. This was the only context in which I recall him using the term "old guard."[18] His critics were men of Alan's own generation, but of a very different mindset. Alan was a popularizer. He was Andy Warhol to their Robert Rauschenberg. His critics wanted the scene to be invisible to straight society. Alan wanted it to have a storefront. Forty-five years after those initial criticisms, it does seem that they may have been prescient. Whether one celebrates the mainstreaming of leather/kinky sex, or mourns the apparent loss of its outlaw status, there is no denying it. At the time of this writing, the popularity of the BDSM-themed heterosexual romance novel *Fifty Shades of Grey* has spawned a line of kinky sex toys manufactured in China and available at a Target store near you. In a recent episode of *The Simpsons*, Homer and Marge turned their bedroom into a dungeon.[19] And in a BMW television commercial, a stereotypical "little old lady" casually remarks, "Your grandfather loved it when I wore leather. He was a very dominant man!"[20] This is just a sample. In a society intent on turning every experience into a commodity, kink is trending. Alan would be amazed.

Peter Fiske recalls a story that unpacks the character of the man who was to become "the original leather Daddy." Alan's top-

---

[18] Selby, Personal communication.

[19] J. Stewart Burns, "What Animated Women Want," *The Simpsons*, aired April 14, 2013.

[20] *BMW*. aired 2015.

space was very connected to his ability to be helpful to others and his capacity to protect those in need of protection. Fiske relates:

> There's a very good friend of mine, Jim Farrant, the whip maker from England. Before Alan moved to San Francisco, he took part in the rescue of Jim from an abusive Master/slave, 24/7, relationship. Jim was in the British Navy and got out in about 1977. He took up with a master who kept him in chains all the time, and who kept him in the dungeon when he wasn't working, and he was kept nude in the house, and he was never allowed out. This relationship, which was very good to start with, deteriorated over time. It brought no satisfaction on Jim's part, so after about a year he wanted out. He was really stymied. He mentioned it to the master, who told him, "You signed up as my slave, and you can't pull out." At that point, the master became even more abusive since there was no consent.

> Jim now started to look for a way to escape. Occasionally, Jim's master would have people over to the house, and two of those people were Alan and his lover Peter. Jim just put that in the back of his mind. One day, when the master had gone out and left him shackled up in the basement, he was able to break free and make his escape. He was totally nude, of course. He left the house, taking some of the master's clothes. He didn't want to go to his mother and father's house. He was not close to his parents, and he hadn't been home since he returned from the navy. He didn't have a lover. This was before he began his relationship with Felix Jones. Jim was at a total loss about what to do. But then he remembered Alan Selby. And he remembered that Alan owned a business in London, Mr. S. So Jim was able to make his way from the Midlands of England, on about a hundred and fifty mile trip, down to London.

> He knocked frantically on the front door of Alan's home/workshop. Alan instantly recognized him, and when he heard the story, what else could he say but:

"Showers of shit, dear!" and then: "But you must stay here, and you can get on your feet." So Alan took Jim in, not knowing him at all, on the basis of his story. He knew some of the facts. He knew Jim had been in a Master/slave relationship. He had no way of verifying whether it was abusive or not. But he believed Jim, and believed his need. So Jim moved in, and for the next six or eight weeks he helped around the house and took the dog for walks in the park. Or maybe the dog took him for walks! He worked to help out, but no money was asked of him, then or ever. He and Alan are best of friends to this day because of the wonderful thing that Alan did for him. Jim was able to get himself out of a severely abusive relationship that included the abuse of the M/s relationship as well as physical abuse. It was all because of Alan. He took somebody in off the street, who he had only met as someone's slave, and on his say-so told him: "Come, stay here." He has the biggest, biggest heart of any leather person I know.[21]

In 1979 Alan Selby and Peter Jacklin moved from London to San Francisco, bringing their business with them, and leaving associates in charge of the London store. There were a lot of reasons for coming to America. Alan was ambitious, business opportunities were limited in England because of the tax structure, and most importantly, he wanted to give his boy a better life than he thought he could provide back home. In those early days, and even later in San Francisco, all the money that came in went back into the business. Alan and Jacklin often took no salaries themselves, but they always made sure their employees were paid. Jacklin was designing for Mr. S, but he was still working for the British Railway. Alan saw a better way, and he saw it in America, in San Francisco. Years before the advent of the "Daddy culture" he was already a good Dad.

---

[21] Fiske, Unpublished manuscript.

He adopted the City of San Francisco and it, in turn, adopted him. Harvey Milk, who had died the year before, had been known as "The Mayor of Castro Street." Alan was to become known as "The Mayor of Folsom Street." Mr. S Leather opened shop on 7th Street in San Francisco on June 17, 1979. Like its earlier London incarnation, the SOMA shop operated as an informal community center for the active leather community South of Market. It was at this original Mr. S outlet that many of the products we take for granted were developed, including Shaft lubricants and the Shower Shot. Cleanliness is next to kinkiness! Their flat also served as a research and development site, with lots of willing young men happy to serve as experimental bottoms for new products. Peter Fiske recalls:

I started to get close to him when he and Peter moved here, and we used to have dinner. I used to check out the shop all the time, as everyone did. Alan always, when you'd come in, would say: "Oh, Dear! I have something to show you, and it's on special!" He always had specials![22]

The British end of the British/American Corporation was not to do as well as the American front, and after a few years of considerable mismanagement it went out of business. This was happening at the same time that Alan was having trouble with the Immigration and Naturalization Service and he could not return to London to set things back on track. Although he was the founder of what is arguably the most recognized brand in contemporary leathersex gear, Alan was not always a brilliant businessman. Certainly the more cut-throat aspects of business were a mystery to him. He was a great salesman and his magnetic personality drew people to him. This often proved an asset in his business life, but sometimes his orbit included some rather dubious characters. Some employees stole. Some business partners were dishonest. His kind nature sometimes opened him to unscrupulous people who took advantage of him. If he had been a harder-hearted

---

[22] Ibid.

man and a harder-nosed businessman, these things might not have happened. But he wasn't and they did.

In 1980, the release of the movie *Cruising* brought the underground world of leathersex to the attention of a mass audience. Masculine images were already in vogue in gay men's circles and the increasing popularity of leather as a "look" confused a lot of long-time players. Until that time, those styles had been associated with alternative sexualities. Now, it seemed, leather was becoming fashion. In San Francisco, that moment of uncertainty produced a club dedicated to gay male S/m practice that is still in existence thirty-six years later.

In the days before the Internet, small groups publicized events through push cards, flyers, mailing lists and phone trees. An early flyer, from before the club's incorporation, asked: "Just who and what the hell is THE 15?" It continued:

> THE 15 is a social, sexual and community-interface fraternity for men into S&M, leather, B&D. We were begun by a group of young, professional men who wanted to provide an organization for men desiring to participate in a fraternal club. Many men in the S&M scene feel isolated and not part of a "community" effort. THE 15 is established to foster the sense of mutual respect, support, friendship and pride that belonging to such a group engenders. [23]

An even earlier flyer proclaimed: "Twelve Men Wanted" in one-inch block letters. Beneath that read "by three others to form an elite corps...a leather-S&M/B&D Fraternity." Body text went on to explain the goals of the emergent club:

> We envision that THE 15 will become San Francisco's most exclusive leathermen's fraternity. We will be PROUD. We will be HOT. We will be NOTICED.

---

[23] Publicity flyer, *The 15 Association*. 1980.

We will be RESPECTED. We will be ENVIED. We will be a group of men who will stick together as buddies, providing each other with mutual support and friendship. We will be involved in the community as a group; and we will be involved with each other in private – holding parties and events exclusively for ourselves and our invited guests. We will be highly visible and interface with the open gay community to promote a positive image of gay S&M and leather scenes, participating in sports events, gay political and social events, etc. We will have our own badge and "colors." [24]

The 15 Association was intended as a club for men into S/m. Most members were also leathermen, but leather, as fashion or fetish, was not the focus. It was formed as a players' club, and it was formed specifically to distinguish its members from the growing numbers of men who were adopting the look, but not the practices, of S/m. These were the early days of what was to become jokingly known as "Stand and Model." A third flyer from that first year makes the intent of the new club explicit:

S&M IDENTITY. Not every man wearing leather is into S&M. And certainly not everyone into S&M wears leather. In San Francisco the two "communities" have blended into an undistinguishable one. WE'RE CHANGING THAT. THE 15 ASSOCIATION is established as a social, sexual and community-interface fraternity for gay men into S&M. THE 15 is not for novices. We are not a "training school" for men who think they might be interested in S&M. THE 15 is for men who have made those major decisions. [25]

Chairman Emeritus Peter Fiske recalls Alan's role in the formation of the club:

---

[24] Publicity flyer, *The 15 Association*. 1980.

[25] Publicity flyer, *The 15 Association*, (Puch Design, 1980).

He helped The 15 Association in San Francisco get
started way back in 1980. Alan helped us publicize and
put up notices about the first meetings. He helped us
gather together people who wanted to have a club that
wasn't a leather club, but *was* an S/m club. There were
plenty of leather clubs and motorcycle clubs in San
Francisco, but no S/m clubs. Alan was instrumental in
helping to get The 15 formed, and is now an honorary
member, which I think he's very proud of, as he should
be.[26]

Business was good, and the city was alive with men, sex, S/m
and leather. All that would change quickly. Gay men were becoming sick
and sicker. Young men started being diagnosed with old men's diseases
and began dying. When the AIDS crisis hit the City in the early 1980s,
Peter Jacklin became sick. It was also the start of Alan's problems with
the INS. Even though he ran a successful small business, paid taxes,
and was a well-known and respected member of his community, the
nature of his business made him a target. The carefree 1970s were
over. It was the Reagan years, and the political climate was changing.

Alan noted that he "needed to be needed" – and as the crisis
escalated, so did the need. For over twenty years, he volunteered at
San Francisco hospitals, including General Hospital's infamous wards,
5A and 5B: holding the hands and massaging the pain-wracked bodies
of the mostly young and often abandoned men who filled those beds.
Peter Fiske remembered his resolute efforts to comfort the dying
during those challenging times: "Alan helped Rita Rockett organize her
wonderful brunches, and he made it fun! He helped the Godfather
Service Fund bring toiletries and teddy bears. Never flagging. Always
having fun."[27] Rockett recalled:

Before all the AIDS organizations were formed, we
used to have individual fundraisers for our friends at

[26] Fiske, Unpublished manuscript.

[27] Ibid.

The Eagle. Alan was always asking me, or I was asking him, to help with items to auction or just to show up to help, and get money for another rent party. Rita's Margaritas was my famous margarita booth that I did each year for the Folsom Street Fair. It was my biggest fundraiser of the year. We used to plug extension cords into outlets at Mr. S Leather to power the blenders. And we always had a bubble machine. That's how people found our booth. It was a lot of work, but very magical.

He used to bring these crackers that pop open from England to San Francisco General Hospital for my annual Christmas party. I remember fondly they were called "poppers" and we all had a blast with that. He was such a dear gentle soul and a real gentleman. I miss him so. My kids, now aged twenty-seven and twenty-two, still call those "Uncle Alan's crackers." I buy them for them and say they are from Uncle Alan at Christmas.

I still remember Alan always calling me "Rita Dahhhhling" – always. He made me several leather skirts, a wonderful leather jacket and a vest. The most precious thing he made me was a red (my favorite color) leather bib with my older son's name on it. I still have it.[28]

Alan also volunteered at Ralph K. Davies Hospital, which had four floors of AIDS patients in those days. In addition to his hospital work, he got involved with support organizations, fundraising, and event production. Peter Fiske recalls:

When the AIDS crisis struck in about 1981 in San Francisco, Alan was one of the first people who helped put together benefits for people who had – we didn't

---

[28] Rita Rockett, Personal communication, 2015.

even know what to call it – but who were starting to show up in hospitals, and who were friends of ours in the bike clubs particularly. This was the basis of what became the San Francisco AIDS Fund, nowadays the AIDS Emergency Fund, or AEF. I'm very pleased to be the president of the board of directors. We've raised and spent about fifteen million dollars. If Alan Selby didn't raise a million of that, then my name isn't Peter Fiske! Like an Eveready battery, we are still going strong after eighteen years. Where there's a need, we will continue.

Alan was one of the people, along with George Burgess, Hank Cook and Rick Booth, who sat down around that now-notorious kitchen table and founded the AEF in 1982. The first year, they gave about $6000 in direct assistance grants. Alan was on the original board of directors. He had to come up with a constant stream of new ideas for fund-raisers, and he always did. In 1983, he had the brilliant idea of having a contest for Leather Daddy and Leather Daddy's boy. "Daddies and boys" was a new concept in the leather and S/m communities in the early 1980s, and Alan is one of the people who got it started. It has proved that it has lasting power. It's for those who aren't in 24/7 Master/slave relationships, and who want something, should we say, not as intense, more of a father/son or Daddy/boy dynamic. Alan was one of the people who came up with the whole concept. So, in 1983, he declared: "Well, we'll have a contest, Dear!"[29]

The San Francisco Leather Daddies and boys raised funds, educated, and represented the gay leather scene within the greater community. It was a working title. An annual contest selected that particular year's Daddy and Daddy's boy. Peter Fiske calls San Francisco Leather Daddy "an active, hard-working title that's probably the most

---

[29] Fiske, Unpublished manuscript.

respected in San Francisco besides Mr. San Francisco Leather."[30] It was conceived as a local contest, and never fed into the national or international title systems. Rather, it focused on local issues, and most particularly on funding Alan's favorite charity, the AEF. The San Francisco Leather Daddies and Daddy's boys didn't go on to compete in International Mr. Leather (IML). They went to work.

Peter Fiske recalls the first Leather Daddy's boy contest as the "wonderful day" when he met "the love of my life," Coulter Thomas:

> It was on the patio of the San Francisco Eagle. The place was so packed that one couldn't move through it. It was so crowded there were people outside the bar just listening from the sidewalk. Al Parker was one of the judges, and of course the new Leather Daddy and Coulter. It was during his IML year, and he had given up his medical studies for the year to travel around and do the community service of supporting the title of International Mr. Leather. What I remember particularly is that we were all just having fun, smoking grass there on The Eagle patio, drinking, raising money, showing lots and lots of skin, all the contestants and just about everyone else. And there, in charge of it all, was father rooster Alan with his boy Peter. There were something like sixteen contestants. They had to have them up on the roof over the bar, there were so many of them. It was an absolutely wonderful affair. For me, it was particularly wonderful in the afternoon with somebody that became particularly close to me. I really have Alan to thank for that. His support to me as a friend over the years has meant so much to me. He's probably, along with Felix Jones in London, my best friend in the world.[31]

---

[30] Ibid.

[31] Ibid.

As the plague grew worse, the demands became more burdensome. The post-Stonewall gay world that had promised infinite liberation was beginning to fall apart. Alan juggled. When he became very sick, Peter Jacklin returned to England to his parents' home. That left Alan to run the business, and because of his troubles with the INS, he could not leave the country. He never saw his boy again. It was a very difficult time. After Jacklin died, Alan refocused his attention. He threw himself into fighting the plague and supporting its victims. Through his work with AEF, he eventually raised over a million dollars for PWAs. This was direct assistance: electricity bills were paid, the gas stayed on, food came. He devoted countless hours to more organizations and individuals than can be listed here.

Without Peter Jacklin, much of the impetus for operating Mr. S had disappeared. Eventually, Alan sold the store. Mr. S still exists, and has since become a successful worldwide icon of the leather business world, as well as resurrecting and retaining the roots of community involvement that Alan initiated so long ago. Joseph Bean traced the trajectory of the business:

> Alan's trek to San Francisco was driven by his leather business, which started in England. He did a lot of U.S. mail order; he had a store in Denver because that's where his U.S. helper was. Then, later, he came to San Francisco because that's where the bulk of his U.S. customers were. By then, he had a lover named Peter who was a genius inventor. He invented many (maybe even most) of the small leather devices we're familiar with today (like snap-shut ball straps and cock-and-ball bikinis and so much else). Mr. S was his own store. He had an outlet for his usual catalog of items and custom work on 7th St. Eventually, he sold it to Richard Douglas Deal, who "gave" it to Richard Hunter, but by then it was barely worth the accepting because its reputation was shot. Then Richard started rebuilding it (following his own success building a leather business in Florida) and hired me. We multiplied its success and its holding hugely, which made Richard very rich and made me a

salary that I was able to live on in San Francisco...but only barely. At that point, someone might look at it and say that Alan got a raw deal, but the multimillion-dollar business that Mr. S grew into is not the modest little hand-making leather vendor that Alan sold years before.[32]

Alan often publicly praised the commitment of the long-term present owner, Richard Hunter, and was pleased to see the business he founded in a simple workshop in London flourish under his care. Hunter says of Alan:

> The "S" in Mr. S stands for Selby. Alan was an example of what being a Leather man could be. He was generous, compassionate, open, friendly and funny. He got most of his pleasure from helping others and Alan never felt it was a sacrifice to take time to make sure somebody else got what they needed. But Alan wasn't only doing fundraising and community stuff. Alan was still having sex with boys even at age 74.
>
> I remember going to him when I came out to SF and asking him what's with some of this "attitude" I was getting from some of the Old Guard here in San Francisco. He laughed and said…"Oh, don't worry about it, deary, these same people never liked me either, they're just unhappy about everything. Don't let them get to you. You just do your thing." And so I did just that.[33]

Peter Fiske recollects:

> When Alan sold Mr. S, he made sure that it continued in that tradition of being a community center, being a personal business, where people were not just customers; they were friends. Richard has continued

---

[32] Joseph Bean, e-mail correspondence with Phil Ross, 2002.

[33] Richard Hunter, "Alan Selby 1929 – 2004," *The Leather Journal*, June 2004, 14.

it, and I'm sure he will continue it. People feel that Mr. S is a place to go and not only buy something, but to try it! Alan set the tone for people being able to have fun. If that meant trying on a full-body sleep sack, then they would try it on. If that meant hanging from the rafters, then they'd hang from the rafters! If it meant trying on leather pants and getting your dick played with, then that was acceptable and okay. And I think that wonderful spirit of "this is a safe and good place where I am accepted and where I can feel comfortable and have fun" has made Mr. S into the wonderful resource it is for our community all over the world. As Alan began it, so it has continued.[34]

Alan was proud of his role as a community educator and informal mentor. He was a regular guest speaker in classes in Human Sexuality at San Francisco State University. He would take his toy bag, enlist an attractive graduate student to carry it across campus, and give very popular "show-and-tell" talks in the Psychology department. Alan also quietly mentored many of today's respected leaders in the leather world. He was always grateful for the knowledge and experience he gained in the early days in London with Felix Jones and the clubs, and he was always eager to share his own knowledge and to make key introductions. Leather Daddy XII Steve Gaynes recalls meeting Alan:

> I first met Alan at the San Francisco Eagle. I went there when I got to town in 1987. He walked up to me and introduced himself with a big smile, a firm handshake, a hug – and a lingering whiff of urine! He introduced me to many men who became my friends and showed me by example what was expected of leathermen.
>
> Alan encouraged me to enter the Leather Daddy contest even though a great candidate, Don Thompson, was running. Don ended up winning, but a few years later, after I had done more in the community, he asked me to run again. Then I did win the Leather Daddy title.

---

[34] Fiske, Unpublished manuscript.

He would usually greet me with "Darling!" and you always knew how warm and affectionate he was.[35]

A dedication to service is often thought of as an admirable attribute in bottoms. It is. It is also an admirable attribute in tops. Alan was proud to have been of service to leatherwomen as well as men, heterosexual as well as gay perverts. He treated trans and intersex men like men. He welcomed them into his heart, his life, and his bed. He didn't make a big deal of it. He treated drag queens like ladies, and dog-boys like pups. He served on the International Ms. Leather board at their inception, and was later named the first "Honorary Dyke" by the San Francisco Womens' Motorcycle Contingent, better known as "Dykes on Bikes." Peter Fiske notes:

> Alan is the most non-discriminatory person I know in the leather community. He has a real gift for liking everyone, and that means all races, genders, ages, interests; Alan likes them for themselves. And he's extremely non-prejudiced; for an older man he's as modern as somebody in their twenties, in the sense of being open to everyone and everyone's different opinions.[36]

Steve Gaynes mentions: "he also had a few men he did not get along with, like Mr. Marcus, but they agreed to live in the same small community and not ruffle each other's feathers much."[37]

He buried three "special" boys: After Peter Jacklin, Bill Gray came and went too soon. Then, in 1992, he met Johnie Garcia. They met at the Lone Star and connected instantly. They were inseparable and lived and travelled together until Johnie passed in 1995.

---

[35] Steve Gaynes, Personal communication, 2015.

[36] Fiske, Unpublished manuscript.

[37] Gaynes, Personal communication.

The Daddy/boy dynamic is infused with the notion of inheritance, especially inherited knowledge and the transferal of role. Alan identified very strongly with being Daddy, and was among those most responsible for the proliferation of this fatherly paradigm throughout the leather community. It represented an evolution, a cultural turn. Military traditions, outlaw motorcycle club practices, and master/slave narratives had all heavily informed early gay leather culture. Pre-AIDS, the paradigms were rougher, more emotionally distant. If "Sir" came out of the experience of and relationship to war, "Daddy" emerged from the confrontation with the plague. The notion of Daddy, together with that of leather family, was to domesticate leathersex to some extent. Daddy connects the dungeon to the hospital ward. Daddy is there for the challenges, not just the parties. Daddy is responsible. None of that, of course, means that Daddy isn't fun. Peter Fiske describes the extraordinary virility for which Alan was known:

> I want to talk about Alan's extraordinary sexual energy. That man, who is now I won't even say how many years old, has more sex in a week than I have in a month! He has a succession of dear and sweet boys, most of them – who just love playing with Daddy! He seems to be knowledgeable, and he is knowledgeable. He seems to be attractive and horny, and he is attractive and horny. He's got one of the biggest dicks in San Francisco, and he knows how to use it! He knows his stuff. Whether you want to get fisted, or have ass play and dildo play, or get spanked or paddled or flogged, or get tied up, or put in heavy bondage, or have a Master/slave scene, Alan can do them all. I've seen him do them all! He's got a monster reputation, which he deserves, he's got a stable full of boys, and he's never bored. If he doesn't have a boy, he'll go and get a new one. He has this incredible ability to keep going, and have fun while doing it.[38]

---

[38] Fiske, Unpublished manuscript.

In 1999, he was invited to be on the steering committee for the newly-formed Leathermen's Discussion Group. It is yet another organization that still thrives, which Alan had a hand in starting. Alan was always generous with praise, and often turned a request to talk about himself into an opportunity to point out the contributions of friends and colleagues. As Joseph Bean has said, "A master always takes the short end of the stick."[39]

By the turn of the millennium, Alan had been in San Francisco for nearly a quarter of a century, and in the scene and in the business a decade longer. He was well known and beloved and no longer young. The season of accolades had arrived. In 2000, the Selby Fund at the Chicago-based Leather Archives and Museum was named in his honor. He began to collect commendations. These continued after his death. In 2013, he was inducted into the Leather Hall of Fame, and I had the honor of accepting that award for him posthumously. In 2002, he was named "Leather Marshal" for San Francisco Pride. He loved it, and described the long, slow ride up Market Street in the white convertible: "I had four hot leather boys as wheel monitors, who added to my pleasure as I happily waved to the crowd along the way."[40]

Leather Daddy VIII Don Thompson said of Alan: "He is one of the most immediately recognizable figures in the leather community worldwide. And even in a dark bar, the sound of that plummy English voice reveals to the world that Alan is lurking someplace with a boy."[41] He was a legend in leather, in the community, and at the hospital. He flirted shamelessly, and had the goods to back it up. He was modest about his own fame, and suspicious of the benefits it promised. He was dubious of the notoriety of being "Mr. S," noting that it could be

---

[39] Joseph Bean, Personal communication, 2014.

[40] Alan Selby, From transcripts of interviews by David Normand-Harris, 1999.

[41] Don Thompson, *Spectrum*, June 2002.

intimidating to acquaintances and – even worse – could sometimes get in the way of cruising.

He was the ultimate Daddy, a dominant man and alpha male who nevertheless lived to be useful to others. He was the polar opposite of the S/m stereotype of the lazy top who delegates all labor and demands personal indulgence. He asked a lot, and received a lot, largely because he gave so much himself, and so much *of* himself. He never lectured or pontificated, nor was he stingy with his knowledge and experience. He often greeted other SF Leather Daddies with a resounding "Hello, Daddy!" He inspired by example. Robert Davolt recalled:

> The most delightful criticism of my old jacket…came from Daddy Alan Selby, the honored leather Daddy of all San Francisco and the original Mr. S. He was helping out in the office as I was working 12 and 18-hour days during the International Drummer contest, and one afternoon he frowned at my jacket and said, "That won't do! We can't have the publisher of *Drummer* magazine running around with his jacket looking like that." And without another word, one of the most famous and honored leathermen alive, the top of tops, the Daddy of All Daddies, took off my jacket and oiled it up for me while I rested for a moment or two. I love that man.[42]

Despite his subcultural fame, he put people at ease. He set a standard that others still try to meet. He met tragedy with humor, showing the strength required to exhibit a defiant, life-affirming cheerfulness in the face of unimaginable loss. He was also, as he would smilingly say about others, "very kinky." He was sexy and fun. He had a heart of gold and a will of iron. He had a profound effect on his friends and could have a life-changing effect even on acquaintances.

---

[42] Robert Davolt, *Painfully Obvious: An Irreverent & Unauthorized Manual for Leather/SM*, (Los Angeles: Daedalus Publishing Co.) 240.

Rohno Geppert describes what it meant to have Alan reach out to him as a young man:

> I met Alan several times when I was just beginning to discover myself in the SOMA bars in San Francisco. I was seventeen years old with a fake ID, begging doormen of all sorts just to let me in, promising not to buy anything from the bar…just to stand and look at the men who drove my dick hard. Of all of the rejection I felt from the Leathermen after whom I lusted in my youth, Alan was the first one who let me know I was on the right track, and even once let me know the reason no one would take me home wasn't because I was not somewhat attractive, but because I was jail bait. More than once he politely felt me up and patted my ass with approval and said something casual like "see you in five years after you've learned a thing or two." We never had a deep conversation… no moments of enlightened repartée. To me Alan was just one of those men driving me nuts, but he was the only one who took a moment for my sake…and I am forever indebted to Him.[43]

Alan's story was, among other things, a story of his time. We like to think, over a decade since he passed, that we are living in a post-AIDS world. That may be true, but it may be optimistic. Certainly the world itself is no less dangerous, and none of us are getting out alive. Nevertheless, the advent of antiretroviral medications in the mid-nineties changed everything. Sick men began to improve. Friends we expected to lose then are still with us. And now, two decades later, with the promise of Pre-exposure Prophylaxis (PREP), there is finally reason to think we may see the end of this epidemic. Alan would certainly be optimistic, because he was. He would have liked nothing more than to see his beloved AEF become irrelevant.

---

[43] Rohno Geppert, "Alan Selby 1929 – 2004," *The Leather Journal*, June 2004, 20.

Alan never contracted AIDS. He was a fucker, and while there was nothing he liked better than to eat a hot boy's butt before sticking it to him, there was little in his personal sexual history that would have put him at a high risk for seroconverting, and he never did. But by 2003, the COPD he had lived with for years was wearing on him hard. Even though he had given up smoking cigarettes in 1980, the effect of four decades of smoking had caused him to acknowledge reluctantly, in his inimitable voice, that: "I've lost my puff." He was quite sick, but not many people knew. A few close friends did, and we were sworn to silence. He wanted to go out and do things and see people and flirt with the boys. He wanted everyone to see him as he was: cheerful, strong, and alive. He would have been aghast at any show of sadness, or pity, or to be thought of as a man who was dying. And he wasn't dying. He was living. He explained that he planned to live life fully until close to the end, and that when he went, it would be very fast. He knew when he was going to go, and that is precisely when he went, with no medical assistance except for pain relief. He said, "I think I will go the Sunday after the AEF Gala. I do so want to go to my last gala."[44] And he did. He enjoyed one last wonderful night out, in the company of good friends. Steve Gaynes recalls:

> At the end of his life, he was in a lot of pain from not being able to breathe because of his lungs, which were in bad condition from smoking. He asked me over for dinner with Tony Koester. Kaiser had told him that there was nothing more they could do to make his quality of life better, and wanted him on hospice. And that is what he did; after going to one last AEF event, he went to the home he and Tony shared. He left us after a week in bed with plenty of morphine.[45]

In the days following the gala, while Alan was still conscious, he welcomed friends to say goodbye. "Mama" Sandy Reinhardt is

---

[44] Alan Selby, Personal communication, April 2004.

[45] Gaynes, Personal communication.

the head of "Mama's Family"[46] an extended network of nearly 2000 "pinned" members who do charitable work and fundraising. She said:

> I loved Mama's Daddy Alan,[47] and when he was close to the end I visited him at his home in San Francisco and he was so excited to see me. I bought him some flowers and I placed them in a vase, or as he would say, "vahz." Then we sat in the living room and he kept staring at the flowers and about twenty minutes later with his lovely accent he said "Darlin', that's not how to do them." So he took all the flowers out, and rearranged them so beautifully.[48]

Richard Hunter also visited him during that last week. He recalled:

> Sitting by his bedside, he asked me what I thought it was like on the other side. I asked Alan if over all these years of being in the scene he had ever bottomed. He said: "No, I actually haven't ever gone bottom; never felt the desire to." I guess I looked a little surprised and said with a smile, "Well Alan, this is the Big Bottom scene for you, and God is going to Top you. He's a pretty good Top, so you won't have anything to worry about, but there are No Safe Words this time, so just surrender and let go and enjoy the trip." He didn't laugh or frown, he just looked at me straight in the eyes. It seemed a "moment of truth."[49]

His friend Graylin Thornton remembered him:

---

[46] mamas-family.org

[47] This was Alan's "pin name" in Mama's Family. Pinning in this context refers to welcoming the new member as well as actually attaching the pin to clothing.

[48] Sandy Reinhardt, Personal communication, 2014.

[49] Hunter, "Alan Selby 1929 – 2004".

Those blessed to be in the company of Alan Selby would immediately realize that here was a man bearing gifts, although one never quite knew or understood the significance of the gifts. There was a twinkle in his eyes that glimmered like none other, and a song in his voice that reassured like nothing we had heard prior. Across the pond, Alan Selby brought a comforting hand he was willing to share with any and all who yearned to feel the love of the "Daddy" they never knew they never had. He brought with him the nurturing one might associate with a "Mother" who sits bedside with her ailing child to reassure him that he is not now, nor will he ever be, alone in this world.

Alan Selby comes to life with every mention of his name. Alan Selby is every man and woman tasked with describing him, talking about him, remembering him. Alan Selby is the first one to greet curious boys who venture into the store that bears his name. Alan Selby is the voice that introduces future friends and playmates who enjoy a beer at his favorite watering holes on Sunday. Alan Selby is the wisdom that enables developing titleholders to realize their ultimate potential. Alan Selby is the refreshing rag on the fevered forehead of the convalescing stranger, and the plate of food to the hungry shut-in. Alan Selby is the heart and soul of future generations who see, feel, smell, play and live in leather. Alan Selby is the myth. Alan Selby is the legend. Alan Selby lives with us on the streets in the city amongst the family he loved.[50]

May 4th, 2004. We had been sitting bedside since midnight: me and my son, Joshua Aidan Dunn, the San Francisco Leather Daddies Tony Koester and André English, and the boy (now more often "boss") Jorge Vieto. We had been there for days, on and off, a small shifting

---

[50] Graylin Thornton, Personal communication, 2015.

group. No one was sleeping much. It had been a week since the AEF gala: his last outing. He had eaten his last meal, a few bites of duck from his favorite Thai restaurant on Folsom Street, days before. I held him, and whispered that he would be seeing Johnie Garcia soon, and to please tell him "thank you" from me. He murmured and smiled and squeezed my hand. Every two hours, we slid morphine into the space between his gum and cheek to make his breathing easier. Vieto kept the hot coffee and cold washcloths coming: a very good boy.

At about 2 a.m., we put his leather cap with its silver eagle ornament onto his chest and wrapped his hot, dry hands around it. Early Sunday morning he gasped hard, and died. After he passed, I held his warm, still, quiet body. The animal part of my brain could not comprehend how his skin could be warm and soft, but at the same time he didn't breathe or pulsate. Joshua pulled a well-worn leather collar from a drawer and presented it to me, just as he had promised Alan. It was the one Peter Jacklin had made as a token of their commitment when they first met. Tony Koester called Steve Gaynes and Peter Fiske, and also the undertakers. They all came. The undertakers were two deaf lesbians with impeccable manners, dressed in something like Edwardian male drag: his favorites. Of course. He had buried so many of his own, and he wanted these two fabulous women. They gave us all the time we needed and then carried his body from the house to the hearse. We followed quietly. A neighbor came out to gawk, and Koester barked at him. Gaynes, Fiske, English, and Koester are San Francisco Leather Daddies: numbers XII, XXI, XIV, and XX. Alan was the original. No number. Zero: no beginning and no end.

Two weeks later, in a packed celebration of life at the San Francisco Eagle, I delivered the following short eulogy:

> Daddy Alan Selby was an Englishman who became an American. He was a gentleman and he was a leatherman. He was the original Daddy, the ultimate Daddy, the Daddy of all Daddies, and He was my Daddy. He loved me and I loved Him. I miss Him already and I will miss Him always. However, His passage was no tragedy. He lived his life with good humor, courage, compassion,

generosity and grace. If we can incorporate these characteristics, apply them to our lives, and impart them to the generations coming up, then the spirit of this great man will never die. I would like to say, then, in the words of His countryman, not "good bye" but "good night, sweet Daddy."

It has been twelve years now since he passed. This memoir will launch before his thirteenth yahrzeit. A Jewish tradition that memorializes the anniversary of a death of a loved one, the yahrzeit encourages survivors to remember the departed. In remembering and recounting, we learn lessons from other lives and other deaths. This is the gift and the lesson of history. Alan's entire life was a gift and a lesson for current and future generations. Enjoy the tale! He certainly did....

PART II: The Auto/biography

CHAPTER 1

Leather Origins

There are so many stories to be told about the formation and development of the leather community. I thought that the best way of doing this would be to start at the beginning, and progress from there. I remember a time in the early 1960s, before the leather image had truly emerged in London, when men who were interested in meeting partners who were into S/m used to wear knee length boots and riding britches, and would meet at Speakers' Corner in Hyde Park. It was quite a gathering of the clan, and many friendships were developed! There were groups standing around, ostensibly listening to speakers talking on various subjects, but the men in the crowd were also cruising, and would seek out others in the crowd, men they were attracted to, and after contact they would wander off together and play in the privacy of their homes. Leather bars as we now know them did not exist at all. Meeting places were on Hampstead Heath and Wimbledon Common, large open spaces with a lot of trees. From dusk to dawn there was a lot of activity. Many men found this a really stimulating experience. You never knew who you might meet. It's where I met Felix Jones, who introduced me to the underground world of S/m. These gatherings continued for many years, until there was a murder on Wimbledon Common. People stopped going there after that. At that time, I was not into the scene yet at all, and I learned most of what I knew by hearing about it from friends who had been there.

Through Felix I re-met a man called Tony, who I first met when I was only four years old. We lived in the same street and we went to the same preparatory school together, and we used to hold hands going to school. We were both four, and we've been friends ever since Felix reintroduced us. Tony is a very wonderful man, and is still with us, and still lives in the U.K. He lives in Yorkshire, where we grew up.

The Marlon Brando look in *The Wild One* really influenced the image of the leatherman, which was strongly reinforced by Tom of Finland's incredible art, which started fantasies for thousands of men all over the world. As important as it was, Marlon Brando's image did not influence me so much. It did really influence leather designers of course. On the other hand, I found Tom of Finland's art incredibly arousing. I saw Tom's work when I met Felix Jones, because they were personal friends. Tom was actually a member of the 69 Club in London, so I did get to meet him. Whilst I found his drawings very erotic, I still hadn't totally appreciated the significance of leather and S/m and all that went with that. I just liked the bodies; I liked the look, the huge cocks, etc., and found it all very fascinating. You couldn't help but being drawn to them, and to these incredible baskets that he drew. The German *SS* look also provided a fantasy for him and for a lot of people, even though they disapproved of what the Germans had done. The look itself, skin-tight-fitting britches and high boots, is very sexual. Tom was great, and I saw him over here many times too. I was there when he was made a lifetime honorary member of the Mineshaft in New York. I was there when he was received by a huge crowd at The Eagle and got a standing ovation like no one has ever had before or since. He did so much for so many people when they were just coming out into leather.

My first visit to the States was in 1969. I bought my first leather jacket in America. I had, at that time, never had an actual S/m experience. I guess I really had led a very vanilla life up until then. However, that was to change dramatically when I visited San Francisco! I was doing the usual tourist things, and I was at Fisherman's Wharf, and I wondered why I was so attracted to a boy in a black leather jacket and tight jeans. He was cruising me, which was surprising, as I was not dressed to fit the image. I guess he saw something deep down in me that I did not know was there. His name was Jerry, and he was the roommate of the president of one of the motorcycle clubs. He turned out to be a very pushy bottom and took delight in giving me a crash course in S/m 101. He made suggestions about how to give the bottom stimulation in all kinds of different ways, and have fun doing it, but while keeping me in total charge. I was falling. I went home with him, and after suitable preliminaries I tied him up. He showed me his toys, telling me which ones were his favorites. I'd never put on a ball stretcher or handcuffs or restraints or anything. I had no idea what to do. So he would say, "You do this with this and you do that with that, and it feels so great, and would you do this for me, Sir?" And I said, "Okay. Now I am in control here and you just tell me if anything doesn't feel comfortable, or if you get cramps. You are allowed to let me know if things need to be adjusted." We developed from there. And I played with him for four days. The third day I let him out.

Oh yes, it was very exciting. I had no idea at all of the possibilities because I'd never met anyone like that before. I didn't have S/m sex with Felix, you see, not at all. It was totally new to me. I didn't ever have those kinds of fantasies. I never even thought about it because I'd had no exposure to it. I'd never read any books about it. I knew nothing about it at all. After the third day, we had breakfast, and he asked if I would be interested in seeing the leather shops in San Francisco. There were not many at that time, but I said, "sure." My first reaction was that the prices were very high, and the quality and make were inferior to those that I had seen in London. I told Jerry that I knew of a company there, London Leatherman, which was making this stuff in much higher quality and at considerably lower prices. There were only two major ones here, which were A Taste of Leather (also called the Trading Post) and Leather Forever. Those were the two major leather shops that had a wide variety of goodies. A lot of people are still wearing Leather Forever chaps. They have held up very well. There were also people making leather jackets, but they didn't have retail stores. Tauber's of San Francisco was a very famous one. In fact I did business with Ralph Tauber before he retired. Tauber's and Langley, I think, are two of the best people these days for pants, jackets and chaps -apart from Mr. S, of course. A Taste of Leather had a night store above Febe's and a large daytime store on Folsom Street. It was owned by a man called Nicodemus. Everyone knew Nicodemus. He sold a very wide variety of toys, cock toys, dildos, clothing, studded belts – you know, the usual. There are a lot of stories about Nicodemus, because he took shortcuts that no one should take. There's a lovely story about him making leather dildos. He filled them with rice instead of polyester fiber. Well, he shipped some off to New Orleans in the season when it's humid. You can imagine what happened. The rice swelled, then sprouted! Another time, when his stitchers were on strike, he had a big order for chaps due. So he glued the zippers in with Barge cement. The customers all went to The Trocadero that night. The sweat ate through the glue, and there were zippers flying all around the dance floor! Those are just a few of the stories from A Taste of Leather.

There wasn't nearly as big a range as there is today, not nearly as much. But it was still a revelation to me. Jerry told me that there was a demand here for better quality, and suggested that I make up a small catalog to get started with mail order, and put an ad in *The Berkeley Barb*, which was *the* paper at the time.

I will never forget the way I felt, traveling back to London by air, realizing that a whole new world, previously unknown, had opened up to me. I had discovered that men in leather turned me on. It was stimulating and exciting. The feeling of power is also incredible – the thrill you get telling someone what to do and being instantly obeyed! I was always very active sexually – I was always the aggressor – but I had never had an experience in S/m or leather. It was like a whole new phase of life had started for me. I quickly made new friends and learned fast what I needed to know. It was a lot to handle at once!

I was invited by Felix Jones to join a leather/motorcycle club in London called The 69 Club, which certainly has *no* association with the sexual position that this number suggests. They were established in 1965. The events the club put on were always very well done in great style. The club had a clause in their constitution that there could never be more than sixty-eight members, so that there could never be a member number sixty-nine. There was often a waiting list to get in. They had to wait until someone resigned, passed away, or was removed from membership through a misdeed! Some European clubs were so large that you never got to meet half of the members, whereas with The 69 we were all friends, and it provided a great social forum for me to learn and grow in.

Felix had really wanted to join The 59 Club, which was basically a club of straight bikers. I think there were a few gay ones as well. They were based out on the Harrow Road. But you had to be twenty-three years old or under to join The 59, and of course Felix was already in his forties or fifties by then, and he was somewhat upset that they wouldn't allow him in. So he thought: "I shall do a one-upmanship, and I shall start my own club called *The 69 Club!*" This was a sort of smack in the face to The 59. The name also had gay connotations because of the numeral 69. It was basically a leather brotherhood. You did not have to own a motorbike to be a member like you did in some clubs. We did runs; we did field trips. We went to Scotland to visit MSC (Motor Sports Club) Scotland and we had a bus, which had food and beer, and it was a real party. It was a warm day and the bus radiator boiled over. So we stopped the bus and everyone in the bus was invited to pass water into a bucket, which we funneled into the radiator. We managed to get all the way to the next garage, where we filled up the radiator with water. I wonder how many times that's happened. It was funny. I shall never forget that day.

It was a very nice club. Anything we did, we did well. We put on shows, and we had runs; we had dinners, we had picnics, we had outings to the theater and to concerts and it was great. The 69 had a good reputation, generally speaking. Some people thought we were a bit pissy. By "pissy" I do not mean what we did with the bus radiator! It's a different meaning of the word. It was a little selective, shall we say. MSC London let anyone in. Tony Small was their first president and I was at the inaugural meeting and became a member. As far as MSC London was concerned, many of the members were motorcyclists. We used to have a bar where we met, called Henry's Bedford Head, which was one street up from the Strand in Maiden Lane. I used to go there regularly and it was very friendly. The Bed Head, as it was called, was kind of a businessmen's bar during the week. But on the weekend, there was a lot of leather.

On the return leg of my first fateful trip to the United States, I had been introduced to Elliot Howard, the president of 5 Senses, a rubber club based in New York City, but with members all over the States. I went to a meeting on Canal Street and was intrigued; this was my first introduction to the rubber/latex scene. I was asked if I would be interested in getting a club going in England, and I said I would see what I could do. I put an ad in *The Gay News*. It read something like: "Is there any interest in a club for men into rubber? If so, contact…" I was surprised at the interest that was shown in it. So was started 5 Senses Great Britain. I coped with all the responses. I contacted everyone who contacted me, and arranged for an initial meeting in my house. After that, we used to take turns hosting meetings in different people's homes until eventually we got a bar to meet at. I think that would have been The London Apprentice. We used to hold monthly parties and almost everyone attending wore full rubber outfits. Eventually at an A.G.M. it was decided to change the name, so that everyone would know what the club was all about. People said: "Five Senses is great but people don't really know what it means. It doesn't say that it's anything to do with rubber. You know, we'd rather have something that allied itself closer to what we're all about." I don't remember even who mentioned it now, but the response was immediate. Everyone thought it was a great idea. So was born R.M.C. or The Rubber Man Club. The membership kept growing, and it continues to be active with some of the original members still working hard to keep it flourishing. They put out a monthly newsletter which is very well-produced, and is entitled *Rubberband!* As a "thank you" for founding this club, I was made a lifetime honorary member, along with my old friend Felix, who was the man who introduced me to The 69. Both these clubs are members of ECMC, which is The European Confederation of Motorcycle Clubs, and FUKC, The Federation of United Kingdom Clubs. They have regular meetings, and plan events so that no two major happenings occur on the same day.

The RMC parties were held in different members' homes. At one of these, I met Bill Cornish. I put the first hood on his head that anyone had ever put on his head, and he's never looked back. That's also where I met Walter Wright. Walter used to make a lot of the rubber clothing for people in England. You didn't see rubber in those days at all, not out in public. People came in their cars to the rubber meetings. They wouldn't go to the bar afterwards in rubber. It wasn't done, you know. There's a very big difference between leather people and rubber people in a lot of aspects. MSC London was much bigger, for a start. It had a quite big membership. I don't know what their total membership was, but it was much bigger than The 69 and a fair bit bigger than RMC. There was good brotherhood in all the clubs, and a lot of great friendships were formed. Most of my friends were either leather or rubber people. Quite a high percentage of these people were getting into S/m sex. I graduated into it. I was very lucky. I had very good experienced people to show me what to do. It's sort of difficult when a top doesn't know what he's doing and I didn't want it to appear that I didn't know what I was doing.

I never had any inclination towards being a bottom. I hated it. I like being in control and my pain tolerance is practically zero. I have a brother who I never got on with. I've actually disowned him because he did terrible things. He used to get me beaten at school for practically no reason at all, and I hated him. When I was a little boy he used to blow cigar smoke in my face, which I really hated. And I still have a great aversion to cigars. I get asked by so many bottoms to do cigar scenes, and I can't. I have emphysema, so I can't do it anyway, but I've lost the opportunity of playing with some very hot boys because they get so turned on with cigar smoke, and I just can't do it. It's partly psychological because I dislike my brother so much. Actually, I never really wanted to be a bottom. In 1970, I was paddled by a French leatherman in London, and the whole time he was doing it, I was thinking: "I want to be doing this to you. I don't want you to be doing this to me at all!"

My early mentors were Felix, of course, some of the members from The 69, and some of the members from RMC. MSC London did not, that I'm aware of, have play parties. Any contacts that the motor-cycle club people made would be at their bar nights. I learned a lot at play parties, and a lot of the RMC parties were play parties. Rubber is fairly bondage oriented, because it fits like a second skin, so a lot of people wore hoods or gas masks, and some people wanted to be restrained. I learnt how to do all that partly by watching other people and partly by trial and error and common sense. I think bondage to a big extent is common sense, but you must know if you're cutting off circulation, what to look for, what to do, and what not to do.

RMC was not always sexual but it was sometimes, and they held play parties. I don't ever remember going to a play party held by The 69. We had committee meetings, we had outings, we had runs and we had parties. We had Christmas parties with food and drink and nice social events. Everything The 69 did was done with aplomb and was very beautifully put on. Felix was very much a perfectionist; he liked everything to be just so. The 69 also used to go to Brighton. There was a wonderful man called Arthur who lived there and we would go down there for the weekend and have great fun. He had a very nice place!

The men attending these events would be wearing leather. The style then in England was leather pants, or maybe britches. Chaps were popular in America I think, much earlier than they were in England. Codpiece pants were very popular, too. I wore leather pants, a t-shirt, and a leather jacket I got from The Leather Man in New York City. But I got my very first leather jacket at The Marquis de Suede. It lasted me for years and years. The one I wear most at the moment was made by Mr. S, of course, as are all of the clothes I have now. There was a place in London, called Lewis Leathers, where a lot of people got their boots. It was a shop that sold mainly to the straight biker community. That's where I got my first boots. That's where most biker boots came from. Good boots, too! And I did business with them, as well. I supplied them with motorcycle caps, which originally we made out of sailcloth, before developing in leather. They had very good stock. Muir caps were not available in Europe then, but they were very much available here. I personally did not like the Muir caps, but they were popular, so I got one and took it back to London and had it re-styled in a softer, more supple leather that formed itself better to the head and that I thought looked better. We re-fashioned the Muir cap as we did the confederate cap. The confederate cap had a bill that stuck out and looked awful on practically everyone. So we changed the shape of that, too. We developed a lot of the styles so that they look better, so that there is more of a sexual thrust to the look.

I was an active member of three clubs in England: RMC, The 69 Club, and MSC London. I had quite a lot of activities with those clubs. We didn't do benefits in those days because we were pre-AIDS. But there was such a scene; it was really easy to meet people in London in those days! There was The Catacombs and The Place. Those were two that I remember that were centers for picking people up. The owners of The Catacombs were into leather, but there wasn't a strictly leather clientele. It was very mixed. The Roulette bar was leather and the rest were mixed. At The Place you could meet interesting people. There was also a little club meeting house under Charing Cross Station, started by a boy whose name I've totally forgotten. I didn't go there very often. Later on, there was Heaven & Hell, a leather disco. That was at some time in the '70s. Of course there was The Rotters Café on the A-40, but that was mostly straight. This was before ECMC, and there was no FUKC, either. That came later. I was happy in all of them, actually. There were differences between the three clubs, but I got a lot of pleasure from them all. We had a great camaraderie, you know. We had lots of parties that I would probably never have got to if I hadn't been a member. I learned a lot very quickly from my fellow club members, and this helped me in later years to pass on advice to novices who often came to me with challenging questions.

So, after returning to London, I started working on a range of leather clothing and accessories that I thought would interest Americans. I produced my very first catalog, and came up with the name Mr. S, which captured many people's imagination, and soon catalog requests started coming in, followed by orders. I was very pleased indeed, as I really hated the job I had as a textile representative and wanted my own business. I was so happy to be able to quit that job, as so many orders were coming in for leather. I could devote my full time to the growth of my own company – and did it grow! I had been a textile representative for sixteen years and I sold not only bulk fabrics on behalf of companies, but also finished clothing. My father had also been in the textile business, so I knew quality and I knew something about manufacture. I went to Bradford Technical College for textiles, so I learned all about textile design, and manufacture. I really went into it quite deeply, so I can tell when something is well-made and when something is shoddy.

One day I received a catalog request, quickly followed by an order, from a man called Mark Wayman. I sent it off, and back came a cablegram asking if I was interested in American representation. This was just what I had been waiting for. So was formed Stage Coach Leathers. Mark made copies of my catalogs, put ads in local gay papers, and things really started to roll. I crossed the Atlantic twice a year, and started calling on stores that sold leather and casual-wear. I opened many accounts in different cities, and all the store owners became personal friends of mine.

Next I met the owners of a leather manufacturing company called SM International. They were Mr. Alex Shanks and Mr. Brian Murphy. I became a co-director, and I incorporated their products with the ones I was already distributing. I hadn't actually been manufacturing anything myself up until that time. We started a small factory in London, and we doubled the number of items in the catalog. They had a fairly full range of clothing: t-shirts, tank tops, shorts, jeans, chaps, and some harnesses and toys. They were slowly expanding their range. Our big thing at that time, which was very popular both in England and here, was codpiece-front pants, which were comparatively new in the gay leather world. They had gained enormous popularity because they showed such a big basket – and of course, being a meat-conscious society, it did attract attention, and it was a great aid to cruising. We did very well with codpiece pants, very well. So that was one of the things that I concentrated on first. And then we started gradually adding more lines to the range. We tried different products out, and if they worked we'd make more, and if they didn't work, we'd go on to something else. It was partly trial and error to get the range exactly the way we wanted it.

I have tried blotting Shanks' memory out because he was such a nightmare. He ripped me off royally. He drank. He was a drunk and a druggie. I gave him every opportunity to be very successful, and he stole from me. Nigel Frost and Eddie Hewitt, who I left in charge of the British arm of Mr. S when I left England, also ripped me. There were some unfortunate situations. There were those awful people who had the shop next to The Coalmine who made my life a total hell. They were terrible, and Alex Shanks joined in with them against me. I've had some wonderful ups, but I've also had some pretty bad downs.

It was around this time that I met my first partner, Peter Jacklin. One day, I was going for a walk down King's Road, Chelsea. There used to be a late-night coffee place called The Place near World's End, and he was standing in the street. I guess he'd just come out of the café. We cruised each other and I said hello. I can get quite aggressive, particularly when I'm horny. So Peter came home with me. I lived very close. If I had been as I am now, I probably wouldn't have looked at him twice, 'cause he was fairly gaily dressed in purple pants and an orange shirt or something like that. He was only about twenty-three when I met him. He was working for the British Railways at that time. He joined me as co-director of Mr. S, and played an enormously important role in the development of the company. I think that if I had not met Peter, Mr. S would never have become what it became, so I owe him an enormous amount. I do. His talent was tremendous. He was very difficult to live with, but very good to work with. He was generous to a fault. He had a very kind nature, and I miss him still. You might think I converted him, but I'm not sure whether I converted him or he converted me. Of course I had met Jerry in San Francisco before I met Peter, so I'd already started on the road, but I hadn't really gotten fully into that clique yet. He got into it fairly fast, actually, once he moved in with me. I was already wearing leather then. Once he moved in, he wanted to conform, so he stopped wearing the bright, loud clothes and the disco stuff and all that. He bought himself a motorcycle jacket and some boots and he slid into it very comfortably, actually. He also became a very heavy-duty bottom, much heavier than I was as a top after a while. In fact, I used to send him to other masters who were more heavy-duty than me so that he could get what he needed sometimes, because working with him all day we sometimes suffered from over-exposure. It was not always easy to do a heavy S/m scene with someone who you'd been working with all day, and he liked to roam around anyway. We did not have a monogamous relationship at all. It would have been impossible, anyway.

Peter was a great craftsman and designer. In 1973, I gave up my job as a textile representative, and became a full time purveyor of leather goodies and casual wear for men and women. It was truly amazing how quickly doors opened for me. I received orders at every company I showed the range to, so I knew right away that I was on track. Peter became production manager of Mr. S. He designed many of the classic harnesses and toys that are as popular today as they were the day we first started making them. Sammy McCarthy was our foreman. He did the stitching and ran the factory. He was the only one of the three of us who was actually experienced on the manufacturing end. He'd done factory work before, so although he hadn't done exactly what we were doing, he'd done something similar. So he was able to give us a lot of advice, which was invaluable at the time. We began Mr. S Products in a fairly small way, Peter and I packing parcels in the front room of our flat in Fulham, London. However, things moved swiftly once we were known. The name Mr. S became very familiar to the leather and S/m communities, and to leather stores around the states, as well as to mail order companies. I traveled to every major city where I was told there were stores that might be interested in Mr. S Products. We became Mr. S Leather later. Peter was a genius, no question. As a designer and a craftsman he made beautiful, beautiful stuff. His work was immaculate. His studded patterns were extraordinary, and I think that he made the best studded belts of anyone in the United States. There were other people making studded belts, but most of them were poorly backed, whereas ours always were nicely finished and the quality of the leather was really outstanding. Peter was a hard worker and intelligent and dedicated. He absolutely loved the work, which was important. I think for something like that, you really have to love it, because you do not make a fortune out of the leather business – I can very much attest to that. It's very hard work but it's wonderful, stimulating and exciting, and you get to meet the most incredible people. Almost all the well-known names within the leather community were customers and personal friends. That was great, and it was also international. I did a huge business in Germany, in France, and in Holland, as well as the States. Huge. I had my catalog in three different languages at one time.

I found a company in London that was run by Vivienne Westwood, the woman who started the Sex Pistols. She ran a store called Sex on King's Road, and she made opera pumps up to size 13. I got huge orders from a man who re-sold them to truck drivers and construction workers – up to size 13 in opera pumps, yes. We did a huge business in those. I also sold a line of exotic women's lingerie, which I also got from a company in London. It was not leather, of course, it was satin and taffeta. Men's swimwear I did, too. I did quite a varied range at one time, and I narrowed it down more to leather and wet-look-only later; but I started off selling anything I could sell.

One man, who was really a character, asked me to meet him in a men's health club. He was standing in a fountain, and reeled off an order, he in the nude and me in a towel balancing an order pad, writing as fast as I could. That was the strangest experience I ever had taking an order, but it was the only time I had to do that. We did build up a big business relationship, which lasted for many years.

CHAPTER 2

Travels in America

I was introduced to two sisters who ran a gay casual clothing store at Fire Island's Cherry Grove. I used to visit them in their home in New Jersey, and they would ask me to model the range of men's casual and swimwear for them! I had never done that before, never considered myself a model, but . . . anything to get an order! So I did, and had fun with it, and did a lot of business with them and really loved Fire Island. The very first time I went to Fire Island, I had not yet fully entered the wonder-world of S/m and Leather. That was my first trip to the States in 1969. I will never forget this hot man jumping out from behind a bush while I was exploring and cruising the boardwalks. He was in leather from head to foot, and said to me: "Are you into weird sex?" I had not a clue what he meant, and thought maybe this was not a good idea. Later, when all became clear, I realized the great experience that I may have missed. But you can always be wise after the event!

I had never been anywhere like Fire Island in my life. When you got off the ferry from Sayville, reality was left behind, and it was party time twenty-four hours a day, if you wanted it. The parties were seemingly endless, and varied in character from heavy-duty leather to drag. The beach with its soft golden sands was full of the best looking, hottest collection of men you could ever wish to see anywhere, and the cruising never stopped. I was invited to stay in the house of a friend from New York. Most of the houses had really wild names; the one I stayed in was called Spank You Very Much! I always got a kick out of that name. There are no roads on the island; it is all boardwalks. At the end of one was a wooded area known as The Meat Rack. The trees were painted white so you would not walk into them in the dark. Before entering, there was a sign in white paint on the boardwalk, with letters three inches high which read: "Gays only beyond this point." From dawn to dusk, there was constant action of every kind; it was really easy to meet hot men. You could either do your thing there, or go home and play. I remember meeting a guy who lived in a house called Dennis and the Wolf. The Wolf was out for the night, and Dennis and I had a fun time. The verbal play was wonderful and he was very inspiring. I wish that I'd had a tape recorder! One of the gay motorcycle clubs had a house there called Aries, and around the corner from them was the House of Pain, which faced the sea. It was run by some of the guys from the Black and Blue Club of New York, which goes way back. Cherry Grove is where the fun was. The elegant people went to the Pines. Leather only came out at night, of course, because it was too hot during the day to wear it. You didn't see people running around in leather shorts and things either. At night, of course, everyone was partying and there would be people tied to trees, others doing water sports, some whipping and flogging each other, the works. You found what you found. It was a very busy area. I was very highly sexed; I loved sex. I could come nine times a night in those days, and often did!

I wasn't actually living in the States for most of the time I used to go to Cherry Grove. I would go twice, maybe three times a year from England for each of the major seasons: spring, summer and winter. I did a very big business in New York. Fall was not so important from a fashion point of view, so I would come over three times a year to set the advance season's range with my biggest companies. There was Leather 'n' Things on 18th Street in San Francisco: I made practically everything they sold apart from custom stuff. So I spent time with them. The big thing was setting the swimwear ranges, of course, because I did a huge swimwear business, both in Lycra and in the wet-look nylon. The wet-look nylon looked like leather when it was on, and everyone loved it. It stretched across the body so you could wear it fairly tight. It fit where it touched and it touched where it fit, so it showed a huge basket, and if you had nice buns they really looked edible. They showed off a good body to its very best. Of course the bodies on Fire Island were spectacular. They were all boys from the gym and they worked out several times a week and had beautiful pecs, beautiful abs, the whole bit, and I really catered to that. We dressed a lot of people for contests or for cruising or to go to the disco. It was really great to get orders from people I'd only read about in magazines and never met, and then I'd finally get to meet them. People like Etienne – he was a wonderful man who I liked a great deal. I made the last leather shirt he ever wore.

There was Fancy from Delancey – I love that name – that was run by two very good friends of mine who are into S/m, and very heavy into jockstraps. I used to make jockstraps in around fourteen different colors. Dyed jocks were a very big fashion at one time. That seems to have gone off these days, but back then we did it like a color code in addition to bandanas. If you're wearing chaps and a jock, there's nowhere to put a bandana anyway. So if you wore a red jock everyone knew you were into fisting. And then if you had your keys on the left or the right, everyone knew what position you were looking for. This was before we published the code.

At Cherry Grove, I met some really wonderful people, and made lasting friendships, including Bill and Duane, the owners of the famed Pleasure Chest. They started their business about the same time I started mine. I always stayed with them in their home in Greenwich Village. I used to take their huge dog Eric, a German shepherd, for walks. When he wanted a walk, there was no way you could sleep, and he slept in the basement with me. I always felt really safe on the street with Eric, and we became very fond of each other! I had been mugged once in New York. – not a comfortable feeling. It was scary. Thank god they were wearing tennis shoes, so when they kicked me it was not bad. They did not want to rob me, they just objected to a leather jacket being worn by someone on their block. This was on 9th Avenue between 15th and 16th Streets by the projects. However, I managed to blow their minds. I looked up at the muggers, with blood pouring out of my nose, and in my best English accent said: "Is *this* the welcome you usually give to British tourists?" They split really fast!

The Pleasure Chest became very successful, and they opened branches in several cities. I did business with all of them. They had two stores, plus a wholesale manufacturing company in New York, and stores in Philadelphia, Washington D.C., Chicago, Key West, and Los Angeles. In Los Angeles I stayed with Jerry Coombs, who owned the branch there. I especially liked the store in the Georgetown neighborhood of Washington D.C. It was run by Duane's cousin C.C., who was wonderful, and always very warm and friendly to me. There was a great seafood restaurant, which was by the side of a canal, under the store. The food was out of this world, and we always went there for lunch when I visited the store to show them new lines.

I did a huge business with The Leather Rack, and I stayed with Don and Richard, who also owned The D.C. Eagle. In Philadelphia I stayed with the man who owned Levi Leather Rack on Spruce Street, which later became Trailblazers. In Houston I stayed with Homer Jones, who owned The Manhole. I also did business with three other companies in Houston. In Chicago it was always either very hot or very cold, so I didn't really like to stay in Chicago. I did a big business with Male Hide Leathers. I didn't have any other customers in Chicago though, so I moved on to the next city. I went to Boston. I did business with a couple of companies in Boston. It was really quite an education! I went to Detroit. I did business with the Interchange on Holden in Detroit, and I stayed with the owners of the bar, and they looked after me like royalty. In San Francisco I stayed with Ron Ernst, who now owns Jaguar, but who was then the owner of Leather 'n' Things. We're still on very friendly terms.

I will never forget my first visit to Las Vegas; I never went to a place like that in my life. I don't believe there is anywhere similar in the world: it is really unique. I was introduced to the owner of a chain of sex/book stores called Talk of the Town; they had nine branches in Las Vegas and one in Reno. He was an important man in the sex business and a great contact for me. I did a huge business with them and also got many referrals. I got to know the company so well that I used to check their stock and write my own order for whatever they needed. They had complete confidence in my judgment of what would sell, and I did not let them down! They were indeed my valued customers.

I remember they took me to a fantastic restaurant called Jubilation in Las Vegas. Paul Anka owned it, and the food and service were faultless. In our company at dinner was an amazing dominatrix, Mistress Nancy, the first one I had ever met socially. She wore a full-length, leather evening dress with a wide studded belt, and looked stunning. She was really a very nice woman. Later we did business together, as she also sold leather toys. She wrote several books, and she used to sell very nasty toys for submissive men. She made things that were very uncomfortable to wear on purpose, things with rings that were really too tight to get your cock through. I told her, "You can't use a half-inch cock ring to put a man's dick head through." She said, "Make 'em suffer. I don't care!" I replied, "Nancy, you need at least three-quarters of an inch. I would suggest a one-inch. You know there's a difference between pain and not being able to get it on, or off. I'm sure you have some customers with fairly decent-sized cocks. I'm quite experienced in these things. I know that you're a dominatrix, but you should be guided by the manufacturer to a certain extent." Well, I tried!

I went to Toronto, on a visit to introduce Mr. S to Canada, and was received like visiting royalty; it was wonderful. There were cocktail parties given for me with huge banners saying, "Toronto Welcomes Mr. S." I believe things have changed a great deal since my visit, but in those days, you had to sit down to drink at a bar. The only way to cruise was to send someone a drink, as you sometimes see in Hollywood movies. The waiter would tell him who sent it and, if you made eye contact, you met outside the bar after he finished the drink. There was quite a bit of leather in Toronto then, and there's a huge leather community in Toronto now.

I traveled to cities where I knew there were likely customers, carrying large cases of samples. I had such fun getting these through customs, but I never had a problem; I had a lot of luck in this. I always arrived in New York. One time, there was a woman customs officer. I noticed that she was wearing elephant-themed earrings. As it happens, I was carrying a range of women's briefs printed with cartoon characters, and one featured a dancing elephant. I said to her:

"I see you like elephants; let me show you an item from my range." She thought it looked cute, so I told her: "These are for you as a souvenir of my visit to New York." That was all it took, and she waved me on! I didn't really think it was bribery. I was just being my normal, friendly, charming self. Actually I never had an experience similar to that. I had other experiences! I was very lucky with New York, and with Berlin even luckier, because I took suitcases full of stuff into Berlin and I never got stopped once. I always had fun showing the range.

In New York, I went to The Eagle and Spike and The Ramrod and Sneakers and Ty's. I went to all the bars, all the leather bars. This guy picked me up at a bar uptown, on Lexington Avenue. I went home with him, and he had a real tree growing out of his living room floor, with birds flying all around the room and settling on the tree. And we played under the tree, and you'd suddenly feel the birds sort of nibbling at your feet. It was a very strange effect! He was kinky, he was a leather boy, and it was a completely novel situation. I've had some very novel situations, I might say.

I went to Everard Baths, which was on seven floors. You would go in, and they'd always say there were no rooms, so you would go to the desk and give the guy a couple of dollars, and he found a room for you. You could find any type of sex, no matter what it was. If you ever saw a movie called *The Ritz*, Everard's was sort of like that, only much sleazier. It was quite wonderful: lots of leather, lots of kink and lots of S/m – everything from drag queens to food fairies to everything. I discovered a lot at Everard's!

I did have one very nasty experience in New York, which I will never forget. I had met a very nice guy in the Rawhide bar, and he lived in a smart apartment in Chelsea. He invited me to stay with him next time I came to the City. In the meantime he had moved. I did not know the city too well, and was unaware of the reputation of the area into which he had moved, which was, I later discovered, the East Village. When I saw the area the taxicab was taking me to, I did not know what to do; I should have told him to keep going. It was a very scary area with drug dealers all along the streets, guns going off, not somewhere you would want to be! I had two heavy cases filled with samples, as I was there on business to show new ranges to my customers. I discovered quickly that my friend had moved into an apartment on the 4th floor with no elevator. I quickly realized that I could not stay. It was a most difficult situation. I told my host that I was sorry but I could not handle the stairs. It was the best excuse I could think of, and it was true anyway, with those heavy cases. Despite big objections, I got myself together, with the suitcases, and descended the stairs. What a terrible street! I was really scared, and it was a long walk to get to a main road where I could find another cab. New York cab drivers will not pick you up if they don't like the look of you. Well, I was dressed in full leather, had already walked several blocks, and was a total mess. Several cabs went by. I gave a silent prayer when one eventually stopped, and I asked him to take me to The Spike Bar, where I knew the owner well. What a mess I looked! I explained to the guy on the door, who was very nice, what had happened to me. It turned out that he lived only a block away, and invited me to stay with him. I was so relieved I could have kissed him on the spot. He turned out to be a great host, and made a terrible situation into a great one, and I had a very successful selling trip. I learned a good lesson from that experience, and am now much more cautious about who I stay with.

In San Francisco, one store, The Town Squire on Polk Street, closed the store for fifteen minutes to look at my line. Gus and Terry, I think, were the owners. They had a staff of the cutest boys. They were all asked to model my clothing, and I received a really big order and continued to do business with them. During that same visit to San Francisco, I found out that a new leather store was opening called Leather 'n' Things on 18th Street near Castro Street. I met the owners, Ron Ernst and Pat O'Brien, and I supplied many of the items that they sold in the store. I always stayed in their home while I was in the City, and they always made me feel very much at home. It became a tradition on the first night of my trip to take me out to dinner in a restaurant at the back of Badlands bar on 18th Street. The restaurant has since closed, but it was the place to go to eat in leather at that time.

Alan with Peter Fiske at San Francisco Pride
photo by David Rhodes/The Leather Journal: used by permission

Alan with popular San Francisco entertainer Donna Sachet
and Peter Fiske at Folsom 2001
photo by David Rhodes/The Leather Journal: used by permission

Alan receiving a Proclamation by the Calif. Assembly
from then-Assemblyman Mark Leno
photo by David Rhodes/The Leather Journal: used by permission

Alan with Gary Virginia at International Mr. Leather
photo by David Rhodes/The Leather Journal: used by permission

The food was great and they had the hottest chef I had ever seen. It was difficult to concentrate on the food and conversation with so many sexy people there! However, we did discuss interesting new items for the next season's range. One evening, during dinner, from the other side of the room, a daddy's boy in leather crawled over on his hands and knees, came to a halt at my feet, looked up at me, and said "Please Sir, may I have you for dessert?" He went under the table, opened my 501s, and gave me a great servicing with his tongue. I was quite blown away; nothing even close to this had ever happened before. I did my best to keep my cool through it all. He finished it off, did up my buttons, came back out, and said "Thank you, Sir." Then he crawled back to his table. This did not seem to faze anyone in the place except me, so I just thought "when in San Francisco!" It was part of my education. I learned a lot in San Francisco.

I used to go to a complex called Big Town on Harrison Street. There was a restaurant, barber shop, dance floor, and leather shop all in the same place. Unfortunately, it was not successful. I never did find out why, but it did not last too long. It may be that they were ahead of their time; later it might have been much more popular. That sometimes happened to me. I produced a physique-themed bed sheet, with a really hot body builder printed full length on the sheet. I thought it was a great idea, if you were alone and horny, better than hugging a teddy bear; but it was a very slow seller. I was disappointed, but you can't always know what will sell and what won't. Sometimes it is just a case of trial and error.

The guys at Leather 'n' Things and I had a very close relationship and I helped develop many new lines with this company. It was with them that the first hanky code was devised and printed in 1972. We had gotten an order in from a bandana company and they had inadvertently doubled the order. Since we'd just started doing business with them; we didn't want to return the order, so we had to think up a way of selling all these extra dozens of bandanas. Cruising seemed to be difficult for some people; so we thought: how great if we could get a recognition signal for what you were into. At least it would be a talking point, because in a dark bar it's difficult to differentiate between black and navy blue or red and orange and so people couldn't always tell exactly the color you were wearing. But it was a way of getting a connection, and you knew at least whether they were a top or a bottom and an idea of what they might be into. And if you thought it was usual for the top to be the aggressor? Well, it was in those days. It was incorrect for the bottom to go up to the master. The bottom could smile at what he thought would be a suitable target and if he got a smile back then he could approach. There were a lot of protocols that were observed in behavior at that time.

The hanky code took off like a whirlwind and spread internationally. It was a great way of starting communication when you did not always know what to say. When you wanted to talk to someone in a bar or elsewhere, it helped when you knew that you were both into the same things. People would wear their bandannas in the back pocket of their jeans, sometimes on their biceps, or even on their ankles, depending on what they were wearing. Despite arguments to the contrary, when worn on the left side you were recognized as a top, and right side, as a bottom. This was a universal recognition signal. There were about twelve colors to start with: red, black, navy blue, gray, orange, yellow, brown, green, purple, light blue…light blue was very popular! We worked together deciding which colors were going to represent what. A few were already in use informally.

San Francisco was the most amazing city I had ever visited; you never knew what to expect. People would not be walking, as you see them nowadays, of course, down in the Castro District in the middle of the day wearing leather. But Folsom Street between 8th and 9th Streets was known as Miracle Mile and you would hardly see anyone NOT wearing leather on that block, which is where I lived. But it was much more of a night thing, not a day thing at all. One day I got on a bus wearing leather and the driver would not accept my fare. He gave me his phone number instead! I called and we met after he finished work, and I had a great time with him. I fucked his little butt real good. That's what he wanted! In London I knew most people in the leather community extremely well, so visits to the bar were often social rather than cruising.

In the States, however, I was a new face, or new meat on the block, and everywhere I went, I made out like a bandit. Of course, I got introduced around. If you walk into the bar and you don't know a soul, it's more difficult than if you go with someone who everyone knows, and he says: "Hi, this is John So-and-So and this is Jack This-and-That." Then you get talking to them, and it's much easier.

I brought Peter over to the States for his first visit. In San Francisco, our hosts Ron Ernst and Pat O'Brien took us to an Imperial Court coronation. I had no idea what to expect, as I had never been to anything like it before. What a surprise when we were called up onto the runway to be presented to the outgoing Emperor Marcus Hernandez, and were introduced as "Lord and Lady 'S' of London, Emissaries of the Court of Queen Elizabeth II of England." In my best English accent I said: "I am pleased to meet you, Sir." Marcus was totally wrecked, and everyone seemed to think it was great. It was quite a new experience for Peter and me.

I started fisting in 1975. My first experience was at The Mineshaft. I'd never done it before, but it was big in New York. The Anvil in New York was unbelievable. They did such insane things there, including stage shows. There were a lot of places in San Francisco. The Cauldron was wonderful for fisting, with all these slings hanging. What a place! The Cauldron was incredible. The bartender used to stand on the bar and pee on everyone sitting on the stools. There'll never be anywhere quite like it!

In 1975 I joined an international organization called T.A.I.L. or the Total Ass Involvement League. It was a great way of meeting new people. They had a roster of names, addresses, phone numbers etc., and a code with each name representing what that man was into. They had a handball convention with one hundred and fifty fisters from all over the world who came to San Francisco. It was held in 1978 at The Brothel Hotel; what an incredible place that was! It later changed hands, and became a very elegant hotel and restaurant. If they only knew what used to go on there, they would choke on their food. A doctor, Dick Hamilton, well known in the community, who was a rectal specialist, brought a model of the inside of the butt so that everyone could see exactly where the hand was going once inside. It was quite a learning experience, great people, and an unforgettable event. Through this event I met Stephen, who was the owner of The Catacombs, which was a private fisting club filled with very hot men, and even sometimes women. Some men found it hard to feel comfortable playing in the same space as women. However, it did not faze me, especially as one of the women was Cynthia Slater, who founded The Society of Janus and had become a really good friend of mine. We used to have dinner with her boyfriend. She was multifaceted, and introduced me to a lot of very interesting people.

I was entering a new side of the S/m Community that I had not known existed: i.e. heterosexual S/m. I met dominatrices in many different cities, and supplied their costumes, toys, and even repairs. While still in England, I met Europe's "Queen of S/m," Mistress Monique Von Cleef, who wrote several books, including *Mistress Without Mercy* and *House of Pain* and a few other, equally lovely, stories. She had the most wonderful playroom I ever saw. She was a great friend of Rob of Amsterdam, with whom I used to stay. I stayed in his basement where his playroom was, with slaves in cages, and it was all very exciting. He introduced me to Monique, and we became great friends. There was nothing anyone could mention that Monique did not have. When Peter and I visited Holland she invited us out to dinner in an amazing Indonesian restaurant near The Hague. It was like dining with Queen Juliana, with all the bowing and scraping. I guessed she was a regular there and tipped well; five waiters attended the three of us. She introduced me to the number one mistress in London, Mistress Linda, with whom I became very friendly, and looked after all her leather needs also. I was now getting to be well known in these circles and was invited to rap to S/m societies in several cities in the U.S. about how I started Mr. S, and my experiences in some of the best houses of domination in the world. I did lots of raps for The Eulenspiegel Society in New York before I moved here. Later, here in San Francisco, there was the Society of Janus. I was invited to Threshold, in Los Angeles, which was an associate of The Janus Society here. I spoke to Janus many times in their different places. I used to go to the S/m meeting hall on Shotwell. It was a great space. I became personally friendly with many of the members because I met them through the Fetish & Fantasy Ball. We had a big crowd from Janus that used to come regularly and really enjoyed it. We encouraged them to come in costume and make it a real party. I also did seminars at the Living in Leather conference for the National Leather Association. Oddly enough, I did not get asked to rap to gay groups back then. I never spoke for GMSMA (Gay Male S/m Activists). Now, of course, there is The Leathermen's Discussion Group. I used to be a member of Interchain, and we used to have meetings regularly, and we rapped to those, too, but that was a very small group. We used to meet in members' homes. The secretary was Artie Haber, who came here recently to judge Leather Daddy's boy.

As trade developed, Peter and I opened our own factory in London and produced our own clothing and toys. That was in 1973. I gave up my association with SM International at that time. With the talented Peter Jacklin designing studded patterns and toys, I was ambitious and wanted Mr. S to become bigger. The opportunity eventually arose to open my own store. In 1976 we moved to larger premises on four floors in Wandsworth, South London. It was called Leather Unlimited and soon became well known. We always offered a friendly, confidential atmosphere for shopping, and people came in on Saturdays to see who they could meet. There was always cruising on the premises. Several relationships developed as a result. The wonderful Alan Oversby (*Mr. Sebastian*) opened a piercing and tattooing salon in the basement of the store. This brought more people in and worked out very well.

It was mostly leather in those early days. But then I found this company in Blackburn who basically catered to the heterosexual kink market, and they had a few interesting latex items. I sold some of their lines, and that was my only source of latex until I discovered the company in Holland that catered to the gay community's kink in latex and had a huge range of very unusual items. We did a lot of business with them. The couple in Blackburn was quite an interesting pair in their own right. The wife wore the pants, rubber ones. They had a sideline renting hearses for funerals, and the man used to see the clients. He only had one suit of men's clothing, which he wore to see clients. Otherwise, he spent the whole of his life wearing a dress. They were quite amazing. They were in their late fifties, early sixties, the pair of them, and they had S/m every night from what I understood. And all this in Blackburn! She tying him to the bedposts in his transvestite state, and they were happy as two bugs in a rug. It was just amazing!

We then started making wet-look cire nylon clothing, which proved very popular, and it looked good, with or without leather. When I first introduced it to the States, it was an instant success in all the stores that ran it. There was a salon in the basement, retail space on the ground floor, leather manufacturing on the first floor, and wet-look clothing on the top floor. I had four stitchers by then. Sammy left us. He was American, and I think he went back to the States. So I met a very nice boy called Bob who became the head stitcher, and who supervised the leather and nylon clothing manufacture. He used to move between the two floors and instruct the other stitchers what to do, and we had quite an operation. We had a staff of about eight by then.

I trained one of the co-founders of Great Expectations. His name was Joe, and he used to collect tickets on the London buses. I met him and he was telling me how bored he was with his job and he didn't know what to do, so I said, "Have you ever thought about making toys in leather?" And he said, "I know nothing about it whatsoever." I said, "Well, if you're interested, and you're good with your hands, I'll train you." So I took him off the buses and put him into Wadsworth and he picked it up very quickly. In fact he was still there when I left in 1979 to come here. Then he joined the staff of Great Expectations, and I believe he became one of their directors.

I had gas masks, which I got from surplus stores, along with rubber street cleaners' coats, and which sold like hot potatoes. They were really great, and they were very cheap. I think they retailed for £20 or something like that, which was nothing.

So much has happened over the years. I have connections in very strange places. Since I had been a professional in the theater in England doing stage management, I have experience in that side of things, too. I was pleased to have entertainment connections again via the leather business. I was so thrilled when Judas Priest's lead singer came to the store in London and asked for a complete leather outfit, which I measured him for. His picture was on the sleeve of their next L.P. wearing the clothes that Mr. S had made for him. He looked great in them, too! I also got a request for twenty-three leather and chain outfits for the chorus of *Grease*, via The Pleasure Chest in Los Angeles. That was a nice order. I just missed the largest order, though. I was traveling on a plane from Burbank back to San Francisco and was sitting right in the middle of the whole group of The Village People. Not being one to lose any possibility of business, when the subject got around to leather, out came my catalog! I was really disappointed to learn that they had just placed an order in Los Angeles with one of my competitors for $3,000!

However, it was still a fun journey and they were really nice guys. I wanted to do more work for the movies and theater, but it is an area that is hard to get into, and you need to have connections. I wrote to every major studio in Hollywood, but got no responses at all. At least I tried.

I did a lot of business with Larry Townsend. He had a mail order company. I met him very early. I've been in his playroom. Not playing; he was not my type at all. We had lunch together at the Farmers' Market in Los Angeles. He told me that he was writing *The Leatherman's Handbook*, and wanted to put my name in the appendix of the first issue, so I said, "Oh, then I have to read this, Larry." So when it came out I bought a copy.

I traveled to every major city where I was told there were stores that might be interested in Mr. S products. One great thing about traveling to different cities on business was seeing the leather bars – the many differences and the similarities. Being a motorcycle club (M/C) member, I always wore my club overlay. When I would go to a bar where I knew M/C people went, even though I was not a member of a leather club in the U.S., I was always received with a great welcome. I was introduced to lots of people, some of whom became good friends and with whom I am still in touch, many years later. There is nothing to compare with leather brotherhood for support and friendship; I think of my leather brothers as my family. It makes no difference if it is a title-holder or a new boy just starting into leather – I feel equally comfortable, and there are always interesting experiences to share. Doing a tour of play spaces has always held a fascination for me. There is a great dedication to S/m by top players, and there is always something new to learn. The leather community has always been a leader in safe sex practices. There is also so much more that we can do for safe stimulation than in plain vanilla sex play. I really enjoy watching different bondage techniques, and seeing how much pleasure both partners derive from the scene.

I used to go to Berlin every Easter to the motorcycle club meeting; it was a huge event with men from all over Europe attending. I used to take a large suitcase of toys, clothing etc., and made so many connections with the European leather community! It was very cold in Berlin at Easter time. If you've ever traveled on the back of a motorbike in freezing weather, you would know what I mean. I met this hot boy in the leather bar. I had to defrost in his bathtub, but he took such good care of me; it was well worth braving the cold. On the back of his bike, though, the wind cut through me like a knife. I used to travel to Munich, where I also made contact with new clients, both retail and mail order customers.

A good friend of mine, Tjorling Terpstra, who was president of the MSC in Amsterdam, often used to travel on his motorbike to Cologne, which is only a fairly short distance from Amsterdam. He had huge black leather studded bags on his bike, and while passing through a check point, a customs officer asked him to open one of the bags, in which were handcuffs, whips, hoods and many other toys. He was asked: "What are these for?" My friend, being quite outrageous, said proudly "For sex, you fool; what would you think they were for?"

The man was speechless, and just waved him on, without asking to see the other bag!

I always enjoyed my visits to Amsterdam. What a beautiful city, with such friendly people, and such hot bars; the back rooms were amazing and full of beauties. I became friendly with Rob of Amsterdam, who made a lot of the leather there. I used to stay with him when I was in town. He often had the most interesting human toys to play with. I miss him a lot. So many really great friends have passed on – it is one of the hardest things to handle in this epidemic. Almost all my dearest and nearest friends are no longer here, except in my memory, and life can never be as it was when we were all together.

A trip to France proved to be a lot of fun. Again I opened two new accounts: one in Paris, another in Marseilles. I had an amazing experience leaving Paris. My traveling companion and I were having such a good time with the French gay leather club, and after extensive play time we were still not dressed or packed. When we looked at our watches, we realized that we would miss the plane home if we did not get started immediately. So we rushed around putting our stuff into our luggage, and dashed to the Charles de Gaulle Airport. My friend had not checked what he had put in his carry-on bag, and was stopped by an oversized security woman. She insisted on looking in his bag, and pulled out his Silver Bullet popper inhaler, hanging by its rawhide strap. "What is this?" she asked. Ron replied, as innocently as he could, "That is my perfume sample holder, Madame. When I travel I do not want to take the whole bottle, in case it gets broken; so I put enough for the weekend in this holder and use it as needed!" She unscrewed it, and sniffed and sniffed, and said, "Monsieur, this is the *worst* perfume that I have ever smelled, and I can assure you it is definitely *not* French!" She then got the full effect, went red in the face, and had to sit down. We grabbed our bags and rushed to the plane. The poor lady never knew what hit her!

We moved to San Francisco in 1979. There were a lot of reasons for coming to America. I reckoned I'd gone as far as I could go in England from a business growth point of view. There was the super-tax problem; if you earned over a certain amount, they charged you through the nose, so you couldn't really make decent money. Plus I loved America, and I thought that there was a need for the kind of service that Mr. S could give that was not being offered by any of the other leather shops. I'd studied them quite a lot; I'd seen what they were doing, how they were doing it, and how they looked after their customers.

One of my major reasons for coming to the States was to give Peter an assured future, happiness, and a great job that he enjoyed. He had been a clerk for the railroad in England. Peter did whatever I told him to, but he was quite keen on the move as well. He was somewhat bored by the English scene, you see, so it was okay. Socially, I was in a rut. I was. America was so exciting – I had wonderful experiences and met these incredible people, and I never met anyone like them in England. And we were happy. We had a much better social life here than we did in England. England was so boring. The English are somewhat more staid in the scene in some ways. They were at that time, anyway. I think the English are very kinky in some ways, but there's something missing in the English scene that's here. It's hard to define what it really is. I just felt this was where it was at, and I still do, I've been here twenty years now and I don't regret one day, really, even though I've had some very hard times. The only thing I missed was my little house. I had a lovely house in Wimbledon, which was beautiful and I was only there a year, but it helped to finance the business. I bought it for £22,000 and sold it a year later for £38,000, so that was a good investment. It was a lovely house.

I never considered living in any American city other than San Francisco. There were a lot of considerations. The lifestyle that was possible here was better than anywhere else I visited. Also my lungs are somewhat screwed up. I couldn't handle the winters back east, and the high humidity in other places wrecked me. The weather here is so even and temperate that it's much more comfortable for me. No, I never even considered anywhere else. I couldn't even visualize living anywhere else, although I have lived in New York for a while. I wouldn't want to live there too long. I don't like New York at all.

I went to see an immigration lawyer once I was here, and asked him how I could stay. If I had gone through the embassy in London, it would have taken years and years. So we came in as tourists and then filed for residency immediately. I did start an Anglo-American corporation, which helped a lot. There's a visa called a treaty trader arrangement between England and America. If you have a company in England and a company in America doing the same things, you can establish a branch office, so that's what we did. But it was still difficult. It took five and a half years to get a green card.

CHAPTER 3

Going Retail

I had a friend who was in real estate, another Englishman, Peter Rowe. He had lived in San Francisco a long time, and he found an empty warehouse space for us on 7th Street. It turned out to be the perfect spot for setting up business. He also accommodated us for our first six weeks in America before we found our own apartments. Mr. S started with just one stitcher, Bill Capobianco, who was a great guy, and who helped enormously in getting the shop up and going. When we started off we were importing all our wet-look clothing from England and actually quite a bit of the leather as well. We were hardly manufacturing anything ourselves at the beginning because first of all we had to remodel the whole building. We spent the first several months, from early March until June, redoing the store. I didn't have any staff to start off with. It was just the two of us for the first month; then came Bill. We did wholesale business while we put in fixtures, painted, and got it ready for our grand opening on June 17th. We lived check-to-check at the beginning. There was no advertising. It was all word of mouth.

Mr. S Products opened as a retail store on June 17th, 1979, and it was a very fun day. Friends came by to wish us good luck and enjoy some snacks and wine to help celebrate our opening. The opening party was great advertising for me because all my friends and their friends came and they were all talking about this new store and all the goodies and the quality, and the word got out around town and people were excited. It's like with a new leather bar: people are always curious to see what it's like and what they have that other people don't have; so people would come in, and of course they would get well looked after and they would tell their friends about the great service they got. So it was quite a bit later before I needed to do any advertising at all, actually. I always did my best to maintain a friendly welcome to customers coming into the store, making sure that they got the service and attention they needed and deserved. I liked to think of it as your friendly neighborhood leather store. Guys used to come in on Saturdays especially, apart from getting their needs filled, to see who else was shopping. Many leather marriages started that way, and I am so pleased that many have endured the test of time. We opened in a good space on 7th Street. This store was at the time ideal for me. It had a reasonably good retail area, two manufacturing areas and my offices upstairs. There was also a leather bar right across the road called The Cave, which was very much an S/m and leather bar and I was friendly with both the owners. They would recommend their customers to come over to my store. So did the other bars. I was getting to know people. It didn't happen overnight. There was quite a lot involved; we were the new kids on the block. We needed recognition and we needed people to know that we could provide the service that they wanted and the quality they wanted at a fairly reasonable price.

This was also a time when important new items were being added to the range that became some of our all-time bestsellers. Whilst still in London I had found a company that made caps, and I changed the shape and the leather on a motorcycle cap made in Canada to one that I thought looked and felt better. I found a company in the States and I sat in their factory with their head designer/stitcher until they got the shape just right. They sold really well. The first cap off the assembly line is now in Chicago in The Leather Archives and Museum. I also managed to find another company, Century Uniform Cap Company, which could make the Confederate cap in leather in a shape that I thought looked much better than the one already on the market.

My next mission was to develop The Shower Shot. We didn't make them in England because most people in the U.K. didn't have showers, so it was something I started when I came here. It took off like a rocket! At one time, it was the single biggest-selling item in the whole catalog. There are very few gay bathrooms that don't have a douche hose in America. We went through a hundred a week to start. It came in three parts. The diverter and the hose were imports that were easy to find. The nozzle was a different matter. It became a much bigger demand, and you couldn't get them in fast enough. It was the nozzles that took the time to produce, of course, because the other two parts were already made; the diverter and the hose were standard parts. One came from Taiwan and the other came from Italy. But the nozzles! I eventually found a metal worker with a small factory who said he could make just what I wanted. He has since made thousands and still has no idea what they are used for! I believe he thinks they are attached to a hose and used to water flowers on decks. Indeed, they do water flowers of a different sort!

I also developed a toy called The Stallion Guard. The actual item, which is used in England, is inserted into the mare during the racing season, so that the stallions cannot enter them, and so make them pregnant. With modifications, it also made a great cock and ball bondage toy. The key part was being imported from the U.K., but after a while they stopped exporting them. They had become too expensive and the exchange rate to the U.K. was unfavorable. I searched around, and eventually did find a metal worker in another state who could make them. To do this took a lot of time, trial, and error, sending samples backwards and forwards, but it is all part of development.

Another important item was called The Silver Bullet. It was a popper holder. I had already produced them in the U.K. and was pleased to find someone here to make them. Amyl Nitrate was very popular and came in small brown bottles. It was inhaled during sex to heighten intensity, but if you spilled some in your eye it could be very painful and totally spoil your sex play. The procedure was to dip a cotton wick into the liquid in the bottle and insert it inside the metal container, The Silver Bullet. This guarded against spillage, intensified the effect of the poppers, and was more economical than using it from the bottle. These sold in Europe and the States in large quantities. We stocked the poppers too, of course. I don't remember who made them in England. It was a cottage industry though, in those days. The person that made them for us here was the same man that was my representative – the man who started Stagecoach Leathers, Mark Wayman. He made the poppers here, and in fact left the formula in his will for his best friend, who is still making them today with the same formula.

I was constantly looking at developing new lines. I was doing it with Peter and even after Peter. He went in 1986 and I was still developing until 1988. It took seven months to get what eventually became Shaft, for instance, which was the first solid lubricant that was also water-soluble. This would have been around 1984. I developed it with a doctor in Berkeley who kept putting different things in trying to get the right consistency. I wanted no smell and no taste, and that took time. It's great, except that it's not condom compatible because you can't get anything solid that is. It has to have oil of some kind in it, unfortunately, so it does not work so well for fucking, but it's great for fisting. It was something I had wanted to do for a long time, as I had never liked Crisco when used as a lubricant. The smell was awful, especially if it was a bit old, and it was hard to get it off yourself and the bed linen. So I found a laboratory that made cosmetics, run by the Berkeley doctor. After several different formulations we came up with a solid lubricant that was water soluble, tasteless and odorless. I came up with the name Frisco, which I thought was great, as it was a double pun on Crisco, and San Francisco. All went well and sales were great, until I got a letter from a lawyer stating that a large German company, called Four-Seven-Eleven, already had a product called Frisco. It was a tooth powder. They said that if I did not stop using the name they would sue me. I thought it was silly. Who could ever confuse the two? However, I did as they requested and sold out all the tubs of Frisco. I went to a patent lawyer in San Francisco to check on the name Shaft, which I found nobody was using. There was a film by the name of *Shaft*, but this proved to be a good tie-in and made the product sell even better. Many drug stores ran this product, as well as bath houses all around the U.S.A.

The business went very well and the more time went by the better it got. Of course wholesale was my big thing for a long time. The wholesale was what paid salaries and I was in charge of wholesale sales, so I went traveling all around the different cities with my samples. I supplied every major leather shop in the US. In New York, Chicago, Philadelphia, Houston, Dallas, Key West, Las Vegas, Reno, Fire Island, wherever else there was leather. The Pleasure Chest in LA was my biggest customer anywhere. If I did less than $5000 a month it was a bad month with them. I did business with a transvestite store in the middle of Connecticut, which was amazing: full of truck drivers and construction workers. It looked like a women's lingerie store with all these trucks parked outside in the street. It was quite amazing. Yes, I'll never forget. I also did business with a company in New York which specialized in doing business with transvestites, and the owner was a multi-millionaire. He wrote a book called *How to Impersonate a Woman* that sold hundreds of copies.

We traded back and forth with the company I left behind in London. This worked well until they started having financial difficulties and went out of business, which made things very tough for me. I had put the business in the hands of Peter's best friend, who I thought would take care of things. For some reason better known to them, they formed another company, and bankrupted Mr. S in England. This other company, which they called Fantasy Unlimited, also went down the tubes. Quite what that reasoning was, why they did it, I have no idea. I could do nothing about it because immigration wouldn't allow me to leave the country. They wanted to deport me because I didn't have the business in England anymore, and it had been an Anglo-American corporation. Peter's friend Eddie Hewitt has a lot to answer for. I saw him when I went back to England in 1990. I met him in London, and he was all over me, but I refused to speak to him. He tried to talk, and I wouldn't have anything to do with him, so I still don't know the reason, and maybe it's as well that I don't. I was still a director when they declared bankruptcy. I lost the money that I had left in the business for them to run it, but I didn't lose any money from this side. It made things very difficult from the immigration point of view. We were separate companies, but it was an Anglo-American corporation, so we were two companies within one corporation. We inter-traded; we bartered, in a way. They would send me cire nylon, and I would send them products from our line that they couldn't get there. Fortunately, I was not responsible for their creditors, because that was Eddie's responsibility. I didn't owe anyone any money.

I still did business with another manufacturer in London until we built up our own production here. Once we started manufacturing, we were making most things on our own. I had Bill as my stitcher, and Peter did the toys, my harnesses and the belts. But we didn't have the right machinery then to make caps ourselves. It's very specialized. We didn't make any caps; they do now. They make baseball caps, I believe, but in those days we brought the caps in. There was the Marlon Brando look motorcycle cap, also the standard one I always had made for me, the Confederate caps and the baseball caps. Eventually, we produced our own cap called the Mr. S cap. We only did three caps originally, and that was only in this country. The baseball and Confederate caps wouldn't have sold in the U.K. anyway. They might now, but they would not have then. In London, it was pretty well the motorcycle cap. And people wore helmets of course, which they took off when they came to the bar.

I liked headgear. I thought that it added to the leather look: a good body, strong features, and the macho image. Tight-fitting clothing – always! A motorcycle jacket, t-shirt and vest, 501s and chaps, or leather pants – which were very popular, both plain and codpiece – and britches too, even. They were less popular here. The uniform clubs liked britches, but the motorcycle clubs liked leather pants. Boots? Dehner's were always very popular. Engineer boots were number one. I personally like loggers. I wear them all the time – I find them very comfortable, very sexy. I like the look. There was a wide variety of type of boot that people liked. There are a lot more people wearing loggers now than used to – a lot more. In those days, I would say sixty percent of leathermen wore engineer boots. I never did. I do now, as it happens, but I never did then. I wear them now for special boys who really like them, but I still like my loggers best.

Some people look really good in caps. It depends on the shape of your face. Some people can't wear caps at all; they look silly in them. If you had the right kind of face, the motorcycle cap looked very hot. I wanted to cater to what other people liked, more than what I liked. I got a lot of my perspective on it from talking to other people. I did have my own preferences, like the shape of the motorcycle cap or the

Confederate cap. The one that was on the market had a parallel bill, and I thought it looked awful. So we changed all that. I found a company to make it just the way I wanted it and they sold like hot potatoes.

I used to go to leather bars all over the country and all over Europe. I met people everywhere. I used to read all the magazines. Of course I'd read *Drummer*. I got very friendly with the owners when they first started in LA. In fact, I went around with their delivery van, so I got it from many different angles. I got it from my own – I have quite a sense of style regarding what I think looks good on people, and of course I paid attention to other people's innovations as well.

After a while we outgrew the building on 7th Street. In addition, the porch on the property behind it was condemned. They had construction workers who did not speak English, and they built a wall just a few inches from our windows. This shut off light to see and to work and blocked the air. Since we used industrial glue, we had to install extractor fans. But there was not sufficient space between the fans and the new wall, so this just made the situation worse. We found a new and larger workspace on 14th and Folsom, which was a considerable improvement in every way. The range was increased with many new lines, and the number of employees grew also. From our small beginnings, we now had a staff of twelve men and women. I started getting inquiries from leather stores in Australia. It was so great to be universally accepted. I added Canada very quickly to my list of customers; I was very pleased with the way things were going.

I had a night store in The Brig, but my problem was that I could not find anyone reliable to run it. I had complaints that my employees were taking people into the store, closing the door and having sex. Or I would hear that they just didn't show up, or that they did, but they were a mess, or that they were stoned or whatever. The store in The Brig – apart from being a promo for tourists coming to town – was a dead loss for me. I would give out catalogs and cards, but we rarely sold any leather or anything else. I hardly sold anything but poppers and the owner insisted that I sell his poppers and not mine, and he didn't give me any commission on them at all. I had to pay rent for the store on top of that. After working all day in the store, I very often had to open the night store and work it myself. I was so tired after working from nine in the morning till seven at night at the retail store and then opening at nine until one in the morning at the night store. You can imagine I wasn't running around looking to have sex, even though it was twenty years ago and I had a very high energy level. I didn't last a year at The Brig: I couldn't take it anymore.

I closed the store and moved to The Eagle at the end of 1980. There was a very unreliable person who had the store there; they wanted him out and they wanted Mr. S in – so it was a very good move. My competition, who had a store in The Ramrod, was not happy about it at all. He had a lot of problems. And who did he come to for help when he wanted to sell his machines and stock? Yes, me. I don't know if he's still alive or not, but he gave me a lot of problems for a while. Maybe he repented and saw the error of his ways. As a businessman, I was too soft. I let people get away with a lot of things that they should never have done, and I should never have allowed. Two or three people should have been fired way before they were. I had problems with staff ripping me off, which upset me a great deal because I was really good to them.

The Eagle night store turned out to be great. We did a huge business, and we were there until it was taken over by new management. I got on very well with Terry Thompson, and I got on very well with Bob Damron, who wrote the gay travel guides and was the original owner of The Eagle. I was part of the family; I went to the employee Christmas parties. Very few people outside of staff were invited.

The years before the plague hit were some of the most exciting times in San Francisco. In 1980 I was at the first meeting for the founding of The 15 Association, an organization that promotes safe and sane men's S/m play parties. That first meeting took place in a building on Ritch Street in San Francisco, with the original founding members and me. Besides David Lewis, who was the first president of the club, Charles Durham was also there. And Michel de la Roche, and probably Fred Vasilinak. David was a very wonderful man. He also started the gay quit smoking class. He had fifteen people in each class, and had a sixty-six percent successful quit rate in each class. Peter had pneumonia and had to stop smoking. I knew he would never stop if I didn't, so we took the class together. Everyone in the class supported each other by phone and it was a great way of developing good new friendships as well as quitting bad old habits. I have never had any desire to smoke since and am so pleased that I don't! Unfortunately, I did not quit soon enough and I contracted emphysema. It does not bother me a lot, but has made it impossible for me to carry on working at any kind of regular job.

I did not become a member of The 15 Association, as I was really too busy and rarely went to play parties. Recently I was invited to be a lifetime honorary member. I gladly accepted this great honor. They have progressed just as Mr. S has progressed. They've progressed very well and I do, occasionally, go to their play parties. I like my S/m in private, really. I don't like doing it in public. There are so many people I know who I've known for years. It's very difficult to have a scene with a bottom with all these people standing around watching. It's hard to get into a good headspace: S/m is a whole different world than if you're just doing a regular suck-and-fuck scene. That's much easier, but I don't even like to do that. I don't go to Blow Buddies or any of those places. It's a disadvantage of being a so-called leader of the community and supposedly setting a good example. If people are watching, they see what I'm doing and whether or not I'm being naughty. The whole public thing really just isn't me. Sometimes I'll do it. I socialize a lot there. There are a lot of people I know who are very friendly, so I go to chit-chat much more than to actually play.

Being a known figure in the community sometimes gets in the way of cruising. I think you're inclined to intimidate people without intending to do so. And I think people seem to think that they couldn't come up to your standards because of who you are, and that's not what I'm looking for at all. That is the down side. Also, some of them will say, "Oh, I didn't know you were Mr. S. If I had, then of course it would have been quite different!" And I think, "Well, if that's the only reason you want to play with me, then I don't want to play with you anyway." I like people who like me as a person and not because I happen to be who I happen to be.

I will never forget my first visit to the International Mr. Leather contest in Chicago in 1983. I had a sponsored contestant, Eric Penigar, who was an employee of Mr. S. He worked with Peter in the toy department. He did well and made the final cut, which is a great honor, as there are so many hot men in the contest. That was an amazing experience. Whilst I had attended many leather events in Europe, I had seen nothing to compare with this. Coulter Thomas won the coveted title that year. It was indeed an exciting and stimulating experience to witness that event. I was invited to be a judge in 1996. It was very hard work: you get very little free time to do anything. Pre-judging went on for two days. You have to get up at seven in the morning. We did thirty contestants on the first day and eighteen contestants on the second day. There was a twenty-minute interview per contestant, so it was intense. And the pressure is heavier than with other contests. I've judged Mr. Drummer four times, but that was much easier. It was interesting to judge IML – the contestants were of a very high quality compared to other contests; it was a great honor to be asked.

Some contests are beauty pageants. However, we have produced a lot of community leaders from contests and the community needs leaders. Someone has to do it: someone has to get up on the microphone and emcee or be an auctioneer and set a good example to new people coming along into the community. Like we always used to say about Daddy's boy, it's not the boy with the hottest face or the best body, it's the best overall person that we're looking for.

We're looking for someone who can speak comfortably on a microphone, who can get the attention of a crowd and who has a good personality. These are all points that we look for as judges in contests. I think IML is somewhat of a beauty contest, but the judges are also looking for an all-around person as well as someone who looks good, because IML goes all over the country, judging, opening events and all that kind of stuff. The current IML is one of the hottest men you could ever wish to see, and also a very nice man with a great personality and a very good emcee. I also thought Tony Mills was excellent.

Some contests can also be disconnected from the kink or S/m communities. Drummer, for instance, is far more fetish-oriented or kinky than IML, because of the fantasy section that they don't have at IML. That's a bit of the difference between the two contests. And there is also the problem that we use contests so much for fundraisers that a lot of people in the community are contested out: there are just too many contests. They have really remote ones, like Mr. Hairy Chest and Mr. Chubby. At one time there was almost a contest every month. It gets monotonous after a while, unless you come up with a twist to make it more interesting.

On the other hand, the winners of IML typically work their year extremely hard. Many continue working afterwards and travel all over the country, not only spreading good will, but also helping producers of local contests develop their events to make them successful. This helps the bar where the contest is held, or the organization running it, and that's very important. It's a very good lesson for new people just coming into leather. It's good to hear some of these people talk – most of them are very eloquent. That's part of the reason they won the contest, because they speak so well on a microphone. It's a good learning experience for the leatherman of tomorrow, who is the starter of today. We always used to say with Daddy's boy that today's boy is tomorrow's daddy, and that's how we keep leather going. The daddy will pass on his knowledge to his boy, who will then in turn pass on his knowledge to his boy. Many boys become daddies, although not always. It's the same with winners of contests. They pass on their experience or their knowledge to their audience and meet people who are new to the scene, who want to learn more about it. I think it's even good for non-leather people to see that leather people do have a great caring community. Leather brotherhood is the greatest thing in the world; there are no greater friendships. I have such close friends in the community who I would do anything for, as they would for me. So, is it the leather element, or do people just do these things for me because of who I am? I'm trying to think of the best way to word this. One hand washes the other. I think if you treat people decently, if they're decent people they will treat you decently, whoever you are. I do get a certain amount of special treatment because of who I am and what I've done, but the leather element is there. Maybe I did them a favor in one way or another in the past, and we created a friendship because of that, and we help each other.

Because this is a relatively rare interest, it used to be more like a secret society, and there was more cohesion. There was a lot more mystique around the leather community than there is today; things are much more open now. Almost every gay newspaper has its own leather columnist that anyone can read, so things are not quite as secretive as they once were. People know what's going on a lot more. I belong to the Leathermen's Discussion Group, for instance. Whenever there's a demonstration the room is packed. When there's just a talk about a particular subject, without a demonstration, about half the number come. That may tell you something. People are very curious, I think. Whilst they may not be hard-core themselves, they're intrigued, they're fascinated. Bondage night at the Loading Dock is very popular now. They do some unusual bondage scenes. They did a human chandelier that was incredible – one of the best things I've ever seen, actually. There were two people doing the tying up and getting the candles placed. The bottom was in a one-piece stockinet suit, then duct-taped and then tied to the board. There were eight burning candles running down the length of his body, and he was hoisted up to the ceiling – it was really quite dramatic. Now, what is that? Is that "true" kink, or is it "just" exhibitionism? Well, I think, probably for the guy who's being tied up, it's true kink. For the guy who's doing the tying, it's probably exhibitionism.

I'd like to see a lot more done to represent leather interests to the rest of the gay community. I do think we are more accepted than we once were. For instance, in many previous years we've been way far back in the gay parade. This year we have had words with the co-chairs of the parade committee, and we're in a much better position, nearer to the beginning of the parade. So while we are gaining acceptance, a lot of our non-leather brothers still consider us as freaky and kinky, and don't understand what it's all about at all. Whatever they say, the leather community has been a leader both in AIDS fund raising and also in safe sex practices. In some ways, S/m is the safest form of sex you can have, particularly if you do it properly. All these people going around bare-backing are not helping anyone. They're making it much more difficult and I'm very "anti" about it. I get turned down about ten times a week because I won't bareback.

We had a flat on 8th and Folsom Street, upstairs from The Ramrod, in the middle of what used to be known as the Leather Miracle Mile. It had a great playroom that also served as a field-testing laboratory for new toys. It was just around the corner from the infamous Ringold Alley, which in the early 1980's was hopping, and there were plenty of bottoms just waiting to be picked up to be played with. It was like plucking plums off a tree. All the bottoms on Ringold knew I had a playroom, and toys for days. Oh, yeah, we tried every new toy that we developed. We tried them in the playroom to see if they worked, and we'd have chalk and we would mark where the snap needed to be moved to or whatever and that's the way we developed a lot of the range of toys. I tried out everything. I had many willing try-out boys, too! They were really excited at the thought of being instrumental in the production of a new toy. We would make whatever changes were needed the next day. Someone had to do it! Why not have fun? I truly feel that one of the reasons for the success of Mr. S was that all the employees were into leather, as well as *in* leather. Customers relied on the advice that we gave them. We assisted them with planning their playrooms, suggested the best toys to be used in a certain scene, and were often asked for assistance in these matters. I lived at that flat for many years until a fire in 1990 in the building next door forced me to move out.

I learned a great deal. I learned a lot about pain, for instance, which had never been and really still is not my scene. But I found there are people who have a tremendous need for pain, which is a psychology that I'm still trying to understand. I understand the bondage mindset and that people are more relaxed once they are tied up, but the need for intense, excruciating pain I find difficult to understand even now and

I've been in it for many years. I belong to the Leathermen's Discussion Group and I've learned a lot there. I personally hate pain, so it's hard to understand completely. It's a constant learning experience: sometimes I just learned as I went along. I made mistakes occasionally and put my foot in it occasionally. I learned from my mistakes and never made the same mistake twice.

It was wonderful making a business of pleasure. To be able to make your work something that you really enjoy doing is wonderful. It's complete. There's nothing worse than being stuck in a dead-end job that you hate, just to earn a living. And I was treated very well. I went visiting all these people and they wined and dined me, introduced me to the best people and treated me as an equal to people like Mr. Drummer and International Mr. Leather. It's "Alan, how are you doing?" And that's wonderful, you know. I do intimidate people to a certain extent because I am who I am, but I can't help that. I still enjoy seeing Guy Baldwin and being able to say, "Hi, Guy, how're you doing?" I don't even think twice about it. I don't think I'm any better or any worse than anyone else. I think we're all really on an equal level; it's just that some are more equal than others. There's an *Animal Farm* aspect to it, if you know what I mean.

Business was going well, but leather is very expensive, and financing the stock and paying the salaries was sometimes a challenge. And I couldn't be everywhere, you know. Particularly it was more difficult when Peter came down with AIDS, because I had to look after him, look after the business, and try and run the store and the bar and everything else. It was really very difficult for a long time – I almost gave up sometimes. Plus, we were having problems with immigration. I was on the board of the AIDS Emergency Fund. I was doing benefits up the wazoo. I was traveling a lot, I was working long hours, and I didn't pay attention to smaller details that I should have paid attention to. There are things that I would have changed in hindsight, but I didn't. My staff was like family to me. Their lovers got sick, and we gave them time off to go and look after them. It was very close-knit. I was personally friendly with most of my customers; I used to get Christmas cards from customers. It really was like a family business, a gay leather family business. That was wonderful, and so I let a lot of things slide.

We did have two employees who were straight. One I believe is still with Mr. S after sixteen or seventeen years – a Chinese man who makes jackets and he's so great. Nothing fazes him; he's really nice. It's such a pleasure to see him. I go down there quite a bit now. One of my employees had a straight brother who worked in the toy department with Peter. He was actually married. Otherwise, all my employees were gay and into leather. Not necessarily into S/m, although a lot of them were. I think part of the reason for the success of Mr. S is that all my employees were on the same wavelength as the customers. They were able to give advice. People came to us with questions all the time. We often got asked how to plan a playroom, what to put where, what you needed for which scene, and all those kinds of things. They relied on us and they knew that anything we sold them would hold up – that if they bought suspension shackles, they wouldn't break under the weight. We built up a reputation for reliability, which I think helped enormously in the growth of the business.

My problems with the Immigration and Naturalization Service began when, on the advice of one of my customers, I engaged a New York City immigration lawyer. That was a huge and costly mistake. He never filed the papers that the INS had requested, even though they were on his desk. Because of non-receipt of these papers, Peter and I were hauled into deportation court twice. The only good thing that lawyer did was to recommend me to a great lawyer in San Francisco. Without that man, I would not be here today. If I had been in a stronger position, I would have reported the N.Y.C. lawyer to The Bar Association. He charged me $5000 and did nothing! It was like a bad S/m scene. They made us sit and listen to eight cases before ours. In each case, the judge said, "You will leave the country within ten days. My decision is final." Bang of the gavel! Peter and I looked at each other. Every cent we had in the world was tied up in Mr. S, and we had nothing to go back to in England. They finally got to us, and the judge said, "We have received new information in your case. Your hearing has been postponed." We need never have even been there. Peter was just starting to come down with AIDS, and the stress was almost more than he could handle. The last thing he needed was to have to go through deportation court. They were very nasty, those people – very difficult to deal with.

Then, in about 1983, a man whose name I will not mention, who was a competitor and was jealous of our success, very nastily reported me to the FBI as an illegal alien. They came to the store to check on my passport and to make sure that I had a green card. I didn't have a green card then, but I had all the necessary papers. But they were not thrilled with the type of merchandise we were selling: whips and chains and handcuffs and all that stuff – it all went in my files, which did not make things flow more smoothly, as you can imagine. A few weeks later, I got a visit from a television crew from Sacramento inquiring if we made the hoods that were worn by the victims of the Leonard Lake/Charles Ng Murders in Calaveras County. When I saw them, they were of very poor quality – definitely not our work – and I did not recognize the make at all and told them so.

When the company in London went bankrupt, I no longer had the treaty trader arrangement that allowed me to be here. That was my second visit to deportation court. However, Senator Sala Burton kindly spoke up for me in Washington DC and said, "This is a good man. You can't deport him. San Francisco needs him." From then onwards, things were much easier. After all, I was employing twelve Americans, paying my taxes, importing and exporting. These are all good things for the U.S.A., but I was still getting hassles. Later, when I got a Certificate of Merit from The Board of Supervisors in San Francisco, I Xeroxed it and took a copy to my lawyer and asked him to show it to the Director of Immigration and tell him that, despite all the problems I had gone through, I did not turn out to be such a bad citizen. Whether he did it or not, I never heard.

Eventually, in 1984, our green cards arrived. But the one with my picture had Peter's name on it and vice versa, so we had to send them back, re-file and await corrected cards. About three months later they finally arrived, correct this time. But four weeks later I got another one, also correct, but with different numbers on the back. I called my lawyer and asked him what I should do with the second one. He said he had never heard of anyone getting two and if I lost mine it was "a bitch getting another one." So he advised me to hold onto it. All went well for a number of years. In 1990, I left the country for the first time since I had arrived to go to Vancouver to emcee the Mr. Drummer contest. It was a great experience that I thoroughly enjoyed, and I was well taken care of while I was there. However, on the way back home, in the airport in Vancouver, when I showed them my green card, I was put in a room, and left for a half hour with no explanation. I thought that I might miss the flight and had no idea what the problem was. I was in a panic. Eventually they returned and said: "There is something wrong with your green card," and I said, "Could it be that I had two?" and they responded, "You should *not* have two." And I said, "I did not ask for two; I was very happy when I got one. I asked my lawyer what to do and he said to keep it." They said. "You must return one of them." So I did, with an accompanying letter from my lawyer, for which I never got an acknowledgment. I thought all would be okay but my troubles were far from over. I traveled to The U.K. for a visit and coming home through customs, I again got, "There is something wrong with your green card." I could not understand what the problem could be, as I had returned the card I had trouble with in Vancouver. Even now I do not understand. Apparently the one I returned was the one I should have kept and the one I kept was not showing up on the INS computers.

I thought that if I had problems with my green card I might have trouble with Social Security later on, particularly if the Republicans got in, so I eventually went to immigration. But I left that until 1999 because I had had such a negative experience with the immigration department that I didn't want to have anything to do with them unless I had to. I finally asked my lawyer what I should do. He said, "Oh, they won't eat you for breakfast. Go!" So I went and I said, "Can I get a green card with the right number on the back so I don't have a hassle every time I travel?" And they said, "Oh, why don't you get naturalized and then all your problems will be over." So I did. And now I'm an

American citizen. I wanted to live in peace, with no hassles. I am very happy and proud to be an American. Getting to vote last year felt really good to me, so very different to the method I had been used to in England.

In the early 1980's, Wayne Haskell in Denver asked me if he could open a franchise of Mr. S Products, as there was a need for a good leather store there. I thought it would be great to have an additional outlet, providing the quality and service that we were known for was maintained. I used to go to Denver about three times a year to make sure that things were being done properly there. It was a nice store in a good area and they did very good business. Eventually Wayne became sick and was replaced by a great guy named Al Dashner, who carried on the business and who was invited to be a judge at IML in 1987, which was a great promo for the store. When Al became sick himself, I went to Denver to go help him sell at The Golden Fleece Run, an event put on by the Rocky Mountaineers, a Colorado-based motorcycle/leather club. Al was too sick to stand, so I did the selling, while he took the money. We did very good business and made lots of new friends at the same time. It was a great run; we had an RV with bunks and hot showers. It's the only way to go on a run! I like my creature comforts very much and am getting a bit old for tents and sleeping bags. I really liked Denver; the community there was always so friendly, and the guys were very nice to me and always made me feel very welcome. They had a bathhouse in Denver called The Ballpark, which was one of the best I ever saw. It had very beautiful decor and very interesting added attractions, like a cave under a waterfall, with a sling in the cave. The whole place was well laid out and had unusual rooms, which were well equipped. There were always very interesting people there. I stayed in Al Dashner's house, which was close to everything – and I always had a really good time.

CHAPTER 4

Community Service

I feel very fortunate to have had the opportunity of meeting so many of the leaders in the community and to have been accepted by them. I really enjoyed emceeing benefits and gained a lot of pleasure in helping to raise badly needed funds for deserving AIDS charities. It all began in 1982. I was asked by Shanti to emcee a contest at Chaps Bar on 11th Street. I had never done anything like that before, but having been to drama school many years ago, I found it easy to talk into a microphone without any feeling of shyness. There was a need in the community to help people with AIDS who had previously held good jobs, but who were now too sick to be able to continue working and who had difficulty paying for rent, utilities, and the basics of life. The S.F. AIDS Fund had started in May of that year with that mission. It soon changed its name to AEF, the AIDS Emergency Fund, to avoid confusion with the S.F. AIDS Foundation, with which we were not associated. Rick and Walter, the two leathermen who started the fund, were in the audience at the Shanti benefit at Chaps and liked what I was doing. They invited me to join the board of directors of the fund, which I did in September 1982.

I stayed on the board of AEF for six and a half years. I was pleased to be invited to join the fundraising committee, and it was left to me which events were put on. I made wonderful new friendships and worked very closely with George Burgess, Hank Cook and Zach Long. In fact, we became the four musketeers of fundraising. I would have dinner with George and sit in his kitchen afterwards drinking coffee. Between us we thought up new ideas for benefits. We developed: Mr. Financial District; the San Francisco Leather Daddy and Leather Daddy's boy contests; and the Fetish & Fantasy Ball. The AEF contests were varied in style and content.

I started doing non-leather events for the AEF. I was getting to be known. Of course, it took a while. I was really thrilled when I received my first Cable Car Award as Man of the Year in recognition of fundraising efforts. I had a lot of help from merchants and volunteers to make these benefits a success. The Cable Car Awards were given partially by the board of directors' vote and partially by public vote. Man of the Year was one that was given by the board of directors and not by the public, and my first one was in 1984, when hardly anyone knew who I was. But that was mostly with the non-leather community. The leather community knew who I was, but it took much longer to get more generally well known. This was the very first Cable Car Awards ceremony that I had ever attended so I didn't even know what they were about. They were given to people in the community for various services or athletics or fundraising and there were a lot of categories: the best poster design, entertainer of the year, or whatever it may be.

Mr. Financial District was totally non-leather, even though we did have a surprising number of leathermen as contestants. Two of the winners were in fact leathermen. We creep into everything! Sutter's Mill was a somewhat elegant bar – not my style at all – but I had fun with it. The problem with Mr. Financial District is that not one of the people who won the contest ever did anything whatsoever with the title. We had the same problem with the Mr. South of Market contest, which I co-emceed with Mr. Marcus. Eventually we discontinued both of those. Mr. Financial District was, however, not a working title. One winner did march in leather in the Gay Pride Parade wearing his sash to show that leathermen do, in fact, work in the financial district. Mr. South of Market was also a non-working title, but always fun.

The Leather Daddy and Leather Daddy's boy contests were always the most popular and still are, which is great. In one of the Leather Daddy's boy contests at the S.F Eagle in the mid 1980s we had twenty-four contestants. We used risers so that the crowd could see the boys. We had to do the contest on the roof of the patio bar because the stage was so full of items for the auction. It was a very successful event, partly because there were so many contestants selling raffle tickets. We sold a lot more than usual and also we had a motorbike donated for the auction. The event raised $14,500; I was so pleased. The wonderful Steve Reiswig, who was Mr. Drummer, came down from Seattle to emcee. He did beautifully in his own wonderful style and really wowed the crowd. He had a great personality with a hot body and face. How could you go wrong with those qualities? We tried a few contests that really did not work well, and some were never repeated. I also had to be careful not to overdo them so that people did not get contested out and lose the enthusiasm.

One day, I was on my way to Sutter's Mill, where we put on the Mr. Financial District contest, which I produced and emceed. I was on my way to set things up. Unfortunately, the van in front of me came to a dead halt with no notice whatsoever, and I rear-ended him, and the car behind me rear-ended me. "Bang!" I bit through my lower lip. It was now hanging off in a very nasty-looking way. My truck was totaled, and I had to be taken to the emergency room at St. Francis Memorial Hospital. I had ten stitches put in. I got off the table in the ER at 6:30 p.m. and had to be on stage to do the benefit at 8. It was really difficult; I could hardly speak – my mouth was really sore – and of course this *would* be the night that John Molinari, the President of the San Francisco Board of Supervisors, planned to present me with a Certificate of Honor from the board. I was supposed to make a speech and I could hardly speak! I just said, "Thank you very much, Sir." He was also the auctioneer. It was so hard to get through this, but I managed it somehow and never told the audience what had happened earlier. It was especially tough as this particular president of the board had a very short fuse and he got bored if things got extended. It was very much a "show must go on" type of thing. And it really *does* have to, especially when it is an AIDS benefit.

I am proud of the titles that I have received from the community. In 1984, Mary Richards, in an article about my life written in the *Bay Area Reporter*, gave me the title "The Mayor of Folsom Street," and this is still used by many people to introduce me at a benefit. I am also known as "The Original Leather Daddy." I guess you could say I pretty well started the syndrome, with the contests. There was always master and slave and there was always top and bottom, and there was always dominant and submissive but the Daddy/Daddy's boy dynamic was not really in place. You could say that the contests brought it out. I really like that title; I think of myself as a daddy in the community. I very much enjoy that role and do my best to give advice to newcomers to the best of my ability. The contests started in San Francisco but gradually expanded. Since I was the title's legal owner, people were supposed to ask my permission to put on a Daddy/Daddy's boy contest or event around the country. Originally I said, "If you do it as an AIDS benefit, you can do it. If you don't, I won't permit it." But they did it anyway, of course. Eventually I let it slide. They were done in Florida, New York, Texas, Seattle and all over the place. We wanted at one time to have an international Daddy/Daddy's boy contest, but that never happened.

I love being a daddy. I'm not a sadist, you see: I never have been and I couldn't be. It's not in my nature. I can be quite kinky – I have some fun toys, but I only use them consensually. It's a very different relationship, the Daddy/boy to Master/slave. I think a slave responds to orders whereas a boy uses his own initiative but gets guidance from the daddy. It's not quite the same. The daddy teaches the boy discipline and the right way of doing things, but the boy is definitely an aide to what the daddy is doing. The slave will do whatever he's told to do, is my perspective on it – but he doesn't just do something unless he knows that the master wants him to do it, and that's a big difference.

I never had a slave, not truly. In fact the only slave I ever had I turned into a boy. I didn't want him as a slave, and he'd never been so happy in his life as being a boy, so I really don't have experience in that because I've never had one. I go online a lot, and I've so many slaves there who want to be owned, but they're only interested in 24/7. I have never met a slave who wanted to be a part-time slave for a weekend or anything. It's all or nothing at all and I don't have the possibility of doing that – it's a huge responsibility. I wouldn't want it. I have enough to do, really. A lot of masters get off on it, on the power. But you see, I'm not power-hungry. I'm affection-hungry and that's very different. I don't want that kind of power. I like to have a certain amount of pull in the community, but that's different. I love to tell people what to do,

but I like them to do it because they want to do it and not because I
made them do it. That's the difference. I still keep control, but I do
it in a nice way instead of in a rough way. I can't help it; that's my
nature. I think there are more Daddy/boy relationships than Master/
slave relationships. It's so much harder, you know, and there are so
many un-owned slaves, actually, because masters don't want to do it.
You need special inclinations to be a master. It certainly is not for
everyone. Plus, there are a couple of other things at work. Some slaves
are looking to be kept and they don't want to work. They just want to
have a rich master who will take care of all their needs. In other cases
it's just fantasy, and if the reality came their way they'd run a mile.
There's a lot of that on the Internet!

The Internet is a jack-off haven, really, it is. In fact it's very rare
to meet someone on the Internet who is what they say and who shows
up when they make a date. I've made some quite good friends, but
generally speaking there are a lot of very weird people hiding behind
their screens. In a bar you're face to face. You can tell immediately if
there's any kind of body chemistry, whereas it's much more difficult on
the 'net. Sometimes I really get that chemical feeling when I'm talking
to someone on the 'net but it's rare. Body chemistry is so important,
and until you're really face to face, I don't think you can absolutely tell.
Even though you may like doing the same things, it doesn't mean that
you're going to hit it off. It's very strange. The Internet is fascinating,
but very strange. But I enjoy it – it's nice to have. It's very addictive.
I've had some wonderful experiences on the 'net, too. I've met some
incredible people from all over the world, and I talk to people regularly
in Australia, Djakarta, Bangkok and Singapore and hear about their
lives, and it's very interesting – very. And of course, I'm quite aggressive
on line.

My only experience as a bottom, the whole time he was doing
what he was doing to me, I wanted to be doing it to him. I knew that I
was not destined to be in that role. Even in my twenties I was vanilla,
but I was still the top. I developed into a daddy. Obviously when I was
in my twenties, I didn't consider myself a daddy. I understand the kind
of philosophy that says that people should start as bottoms and then

graduate to becoming tops, and I think in a lot of cases that's true. But it just wasn't so in my case. I think it's a case of different strokes for different folks. I just always knew where I was at. So I don't agree that you have to start at the bottom. Of course there are also bottoms who never have any top tendencies – ever. A lot. And it's not a question of age in either category, except I think a daddy should be at least thirty to thirty-five to be convincing. People who say they're daddies at eighteen or even tops at eighteen I take with several grains of salt. But a boy can be a boy at sixty. It's a state of mind, not a state of age. And that's the difference – but I don't think you have to have been a bottom to be a good top. I think the more experience you have the better it is and the better you do it. But I didn't enjoy being a bottom at all – I hated it. Not comfortable, not my nature.

Now, I would not use a new electrical toy, for instance, on anyone until someone had shown me the right way to do it. Then I would probably start very lightly and work with the bottom. I like things to be consensual – I don't like to force people to do things. And I probably wouldn't be interested in playing with a person who wanted to be "forced." It's never happened.

I've only ever met three people who wanted that and I refused to play with any of them. It just is not comfortable for me. I don't want to force people to do things against their will, because that's not where I'm coming from. There are people that want to do that; let them do it. There are lots of things that I'm not comfortable doing: unsafe sex, for that matter. People do it – people do all kinds of things. People want bestiality, which I'm not into at all. There are so many different facets of kinky sex, but we can't all like the same things and it's probably just as well that we don't.

Some things are hard to talk about. I think I did the best I could under the circumstances. It was very hard to try and look after my partner who had AIDS and run the business at the same time. And I've wished that I could have had someone that I trusted completely to look after Mr. S while I looked after Peter. That's one of my regrets; that didn't happen. I just didn't have anyone at that time, and that was tough because I was very fond of Peter and I had to leave him more than I wanted to. I had to send him home to his mother, which was a very difficult thing for me. She blamed me for everything. He refused to allow me to tell his mother that he had AIDS, so that was a difficult situation, too. It was a hard period for me: I was producing all these benefits as well as running the business and looking after him. He left here in 1986 to go back to his family in England, as I could not run the business on my own and look after him at the same time. It was a human impossibility. I really hated having to do that but felt that I had no option, and his parents wanted him with them anyway. My one major regret was that Peter became sick with the AIDS virus and never lived to see the great success that Mr. S would become. It was due in large part to his talent as a designer/production manager. He designed them and I sold them: it was a great partnership. Peter Jacklin passed away from AIDS in 1987.

I couldn't be a tough businessman; it wasn't in my nature. I'd have probably made a lot more money if I had been. We never did shortcuts or skimped on anything. Rather the reverse. We gave the customer the very best value for their money, which is why we were so successful, but we didn't make so much money. There were lots of problems, but lots of good times too: very big ups and not that many downs. So that's how I was able to cope with things. I don't think I would have changed very much.

The leather community should be very proud that we have collectively raised – at The S.F. Eagle alone – over five-and-a-half million dollars for AIDS charities. The Fetish & Fantasy Ball has always been fun, entertaining and instructive. The first one was at The Arena Bar. Supervisor Harry Britt showed up and I was really pleased to see him there. From there we moved to The Brig and had to turn one hundred and fifty people away. The place was packed! We had to move it to larger premises: first Dreamland on Harrison Street, then The End-Up and on to Colossus, which was a great space. Finally this year it was at Club Townsend and was busier than ever.

Great demonstrations and fantasies were performed at the Fetish & Fantasy Balls. There were, however, a couple of incidents during these events that were embarrassing to the people doing the demos, as they were accredited experts in their field. One expert was demonstrating the magic wand, which he had in his hand. Without thinking, he picked up a microphone in his other hand and the result was a nasty electric shock. He was shaking and we had to turn the power off quickly! The other occasion was a mummification, inside a coffin, with the bottom decorated with Christmas tree lights. Unfortunately they shorted out and we had to move quickly to avoid a fatality! The human buffet was much safer, and very popular. This also involved mummification. Once secure, the bottom's body would be covered in fruits and vegetables, cheeses and crackers, all very artistically arranged. There were carrots and tomatoes and bunches of grapes. It was very popular! Another popular event was "The Dos and Don'ts of S/m," a short class for novices, which was very instructive. It covered the correct way to use handcuffs, hoods, riding crops, whips and especially bondage. I was told that the Fetish & Fantasy Ball was the most enjoyable event during Leather Week, (apart from the Folsom Street Fair, which was always a mind-blower) and it attracted people from all over the world. This is a great fundraiser for the AEF, and there is no reason that it should not keep getting bigger and better every year. I think teaching should be fun. It should be instructive and educational, absolutely. There's always something to learn, and you can learn a lot from other people's experiences. Of course, that is another role for leaders: to pass on their experience and knowledge to beginners. That's why the Leather Leadership Conference was so popular: because there were so many diverse subjects that people wanted to know about.

Folsom Street Fair is incredible. It takes half an hour to forty-five minutes to walk just one block. That's partly because there are so many people, and partly because I know so many people and I want to say hello along the way. And there are such interesting booths and incredible outfits. I always enjoy Folsom Street Fair – I haven't missed one yet. And of course I used to live right there, and I used to get up early in the morning and make coffee for the people who were setting up the booths out in the street. Michael Valerio, who started the Folsom Street Fair, was an old friend of mine, so I would go down there and meet them all and make them coffee, which was nice. It's gotten huge. Maybe it has gotten too big, but they give away a tremendous amount of money to charity every year, so we have to take that into consideration. Thousands of dollars are given away to needy charities; so if a few straight people want to gawk, let them gawk. The gay parade attracts a lot of straight people, too, so it's the same argument. If they want to come, they're going to come. It's an open, public thing. But I think some people are inclined to behave a little irresponsibly at some of these events. It may be fuel for the religious right, unfortunately. That's the danger. I did flog someone at The 15 booth a couple of times. That's not irresponsible, but I was being filmed at the time and I didn't know by whom. So that was the irresponsible part. But I was raising money for the AEF – it was a dollar a stroke, paid by the bottom.

The AEF was always an inspiring organization to work for and with. I remember at the Gay Pride Parade – and how proud I was to be invited to march – holding the banner with Rick Booth, the co-founder, and still great friend of mine, plus Hank Cook, George Burgess and Rick Salinas, all wonderful men and all special to me. We used to have such a good time doing that: we would carry our own refreshments and pass them down to each other. We loved the appreciation we got from the crowd, and many times we won the Cable Car Award for the best float. The fund had the lowest overheads of any charity that I knew of, and it got such great support from the community. It still does, because it gives back to clients almost ninety-five cents of every dollar it takes in, which is really remarkable. They sometimes give out $150,000 per month. We can be proud that it was founded by leathermen and there has always been at least one leatherman on the board of directors. I regretted so much the fact that I contracted emphysema and was no longer able to march in the parade. The thrill of the crowd's yells and applause was wonderful and inspiring. In the early years we were allowed to break ranks and accept money from the people at the side of the road. One year my partner Peter and I collected $1300 between us during the march. We did all kinds of things, some of them really kooky, to collect money for charity. I ran a Spankathon for nine months. I took it over from Daddy Don Thompson, who had worked diligently with it but had so many other things to do. I was pleased when I added everything up and found that I had raised $2,300 at a dollar-a-spank. However, I have to admit that I had help. And I had certain ways of getting more money than just a dollar-a-spank, and I had talented people in the audience. It was fun. I like doing that kind of stuff – it really gives me a good feeling. I was in the theater, so I'm not shy. I don't consider myself an extrovert, but I like raising money for worthy charities. To some people it certainly is exhibitionist and it is, or it can be. It depends on what you're doing. I think that some masters or tops are inclined to be somewhat exhibitionistic. There are some exhibitionist bottoms, too. But that isn't really where I'm coming from. I'll do it: I will spank people in a bar, or do silly things. Don had to dance with a drag queen last week, for instance. I do what I'm expected to do and I don't feel bad about doing it, but I'm not exhibitionistic. A lot of people love to be watched, and some people are very good. I've seen some incredible scenes that I'm not capable of doing because I have no experience. Things like butterfly piercing: I've never done it to anyone, so I don't desire to do it, but it's fascinating to watch. And I do have a fairly wide repertoire. You should see my toy box! You'd be surprised. I get into all kinds of things. I have preferences, of course, like everyone. I probably have a narrower field than people who have these big, exotic playrooms. I used to have a great playroom, which I no longer have, so that makes a difference. I think if you don't have bondage equipment or a sling, you are limited in the scenes you can do. You just make the most of what you are able to do. Fortunately, I have certain things that I really enjoy doing, and I have boys who really enjoy having these things done to them.

One night three of the hottest men you ever saw in your life came into The Nightshift, where I was doing an event. One was a porn star, one was a model and the other was from the gym. They had bodies by God, with faces to match. Well, when they got on the stage everyone was yelling: "I'll give you $20 if any of them take their

501's down!" They then got into switch spanking and the whole bar just burst with excitement and people were offering $5 a spank if they could spank one of these hot men or even watch them spank each other. Wow. What a night that was! As I was on the stage, I got to see everything – and I do mean everything! It's great when you can do good things and have a lot of fun and excitement at the same time. It also brings business in for the bar. We usually held this event on a weeknight when the bar might be fairly quiet. In this way you can benefit the charity and help the owner of the bar by increasing his business.

I was very honored to be the only man on the board of directors of International Ms. Leather for their first year-and-a-half of existence. That was another important learning experience. We really worked hard to get it off the ground, doing whatever we could to raise funds to cover the expenses of putting on the contest. I was pleased with the support we got to put on the first Ms. San Francisco Contest, which Shadow Morton won. Shadow was wonderful. I became very close with the leather women's community and still am to this day, and I do my best to support their events. I used to go to the South Bay often to co-emcee benefits at Gregg's Ballroom with leather women title-holders. They were great and always very nice to me. I have judged many of their contests and am so pleased that the women's community helps the men in their endeavors and works with us in harmony. Fetish & Fantasy was a good example of this. There were gay, straight and bisexual men and women with similar interests, all there to have a good time, to be entertained and to become more informed. The fantasies were always well done, and the mummified human buffet was a constant attraction. It all raised big bucks for the AEF and was a lot of fun to produce.

I had a couple of embarrassing moments while emceeing benefits. I made two *major* booboos! Once, I had invited a special guest to be a speaker at the Leather Daddy contest at Chaps Bar. His name was Jack McCarthy, and his lover was Victor. Jack had been involved in a hijacking in Tehran and was lucky not to have been killed. He had been going around the world giving talks on AIDS, and I thought,

"What a perfect man to have." I was thrilled when he accepted. I was so excited that I introduced him as a "fugitive" instead of as a hostage! He was not amused. Another time, during the Mr. South of Market contest at Dreamland, I forgot to introduce one of the judges, Richard Rawlings, who was Mr. Uniform of San Francisco and a very good friend of mine. He had traveled up specially to judge the event. A little voice piped up to say: "I think you forgot me." I was mortified.

The only event that I produced that was a disaster was the one that I worked the hardest to produce. This was in the late 1980s. I thought that an adult gay prom in a real gym in a real high school would be very popular. I had to get special permission from the San Francisco Unified School District and have meetings with the headmistress. We had tons of food donated and I hired the very wonderful City Swing Band to play. I had not bargained on the fact that, due to it being in a high school, I could not serve alcohol, nor allow spike heel shoes because of the floor on the gym. I catered for an expected 1,500 people and only 150 showed up! I had to give food away afterwards to hospices. They were glad to have it, anyway. It was just such a disappointment after all the careful planning. I even got a mobile stage lent to us and had Jax Trucks donate delivery to and from Theater Artaud. We were $2000 in the hole. With drag queens, spiked heels go with alcohol. They do! It was a shame. I think if we'd been able to have the alcohol it might have been OK. I should have just done it, but I daren't have done the spike heels. I couldn't really put down a cover on top of the gym floor. The people who were there had a ball. We had a great time. It was a regular prom, except the boys danced with the boys and the girls danced with the girls. We had a gay dance club from the East Bay that came over, and they were all dressed like ballroom dancers. Some came dressed in high school gear with pigtails and ribbons in their hair and retro stuff. It was fun. It could have been a wonderful event and it should have been, but it was just one of those things. I had expected a big crowd. I had the gay cops doing security on the grounds, but they had nothing to do; they were twiddling their thumbs. It was a shame. I had so much extra food: I had the doorway of Coming Home Hospice piled high with cakes and cookies and desserts and all kinds of stuff. So that much was good.

I also worked as a caregiver/masseur on the AIDS ward of the hospital. I trained in massage with Irene Smith, who runs a great organization called Service Through Touch, which trains masseurs to go out into hospices, jails, hospitals, etc., to help ease the pain of people with AIDS. This was something I really enjoyed doing; there was a great need for volunteers and it really helped the nurses. It was indeed very hard work, but the appreciation I received was wonderful and made me feel really good. I checked on sixty patients a day and did about ten massages on each visit. It was hard work, but it was worthwhile. One man came up to me, the lover of one of my patients, and said, "I want to thank you. You gave my partner a massage on the ward, and he had the best night's sleep he has had in months!" It made my work doubly important and meaningful to get this kind of feedback. I got a certificate, actually, so I could do massage on the AIDS ward. I'd already been doing the massage work, but they brought out a new regulation at the hospital. You couldn't do it unless you'd gone through their training. They wouldn't accept my British Navy training, so I had to do it again.

Business continued, but my heart was not really in it without Peter. I had by then built up good connections with the heterosexual S/m Community, and often rapped to societies in various U.S. cities about my experiences. I was asked to supply all the toys and outfits for the mistresses in a new house of domination in Los Angeles. I discovered that the mistresses were mostly inexperienced; they needed training. There were about twelve of them. They were asked to sit in a circle at my feet, and they brought in a man who was told to stand in the center of the circle in front of me. I had to demonstrate on him how to use leather cock-and-ball toys, stretchers, spreaders, and the like. He was quite embarrassed, as I was also, but I got through it all right. I thought it important that they know how to use the toys correctly to have the desired effect without seriously hurting anyone. Mr. S Leather was the first company to introduce women's lingerie in leather, which I think is an important point. I wasn't really happy about the house of domination in Los Angeles because it was so badly run. Another time, I did a demonstration bondage scene with two women tied to a post. I had to do a demonstration of rope bondage of their breasts, and then tie them together and do a decorative centerpiece. I did it because it was good for business. My cock wasn't in it. But I serviced mistresses all over the States, actually, and I looked after all the mistresses in New York. I knew them all by name: I used to go to their places. I was very friendly with the Queen of S/m, who is Monique Von Cleef from The Hague in Holland. She was amazing, and turned me on to Mistress Linda in London; subsequently, I did all her toys, outfits, repairs, everything. They in turn turned me on to the mistresses in New York. I met a lot more through Eulenspiegel, and then I met Sir James of Le Chateau San Francisco, who also became a huge customer.

I'm also very friendly with Mistress Marilyn, and Cleo Dubois and Sybil Holiday, who are all professional dominatrices. I did two benefits for the 1987 Spanner fiasco. That was the case of the fifteen men in England who were arrested for consensual S/m play. They made the mistake of videotaping and the tape fell into the wrong hands. Communities around the world raised money to take the case to the European Court of Appeal to have their charges dropped. I did a benefit for them at Castlebar on a wet Wednesday afternoon. I was the only gay man in the whole place in addition to two lesbians. Otherwise, they were nearly all dominatrices and straight male submissives. I was very well received and acted as auctioneer with Mistress Marilyn; we raised $2,300 to benefit Alan Oversby, who was the tattoo artist Mr. Sebastian, a very close friend of mine. I thought that, under the circumstances, it was a good amount, and I got a very nice letter of appreciation from the Spanner Committee. The Spanner thing really killed him, actually. It was such a shame – he was such a great man. It was a travesty. British justice is very strange.

I rapped to S/m societies around the state about my experiences, and I was also a guest speaker at San Francisco State University in the Psychology Department's "Human Sexuality" class. I really enjoyed it. I would talk about safe sex and get great receptions from the classes, where as many as one hundred-and- seventy-five students at a time would be present. I would take a large case of toys to class, and we had a lot of fun with them! Most had never seen anything like them before and found it very stimulating. I did it every semester for nine years. One day a teacher was sick, and they put "Sexual Deviations" with my regular class, which was "Human Sexuality." I had to park in a parking lot on the other side of the campus. As the bag of goodies I was taking to class was quite heavy, I requested someone to carry my bag across the campus for me. I got the teacher's assistant to do this for me. For some reason I got a great sense of satisfaction from this! The students always asked very interesting and intelligent questions. The teacher told me she always learned something new when I came to class, and that gave me great pleasure to hear.

I once had an invitation to speak at The Institute for Human Sexuality. The room was full of psychiatrists, psychologists and students. I was talking about latex, and many tried to disagree with many of the things I was saying. I told them that I was speaking from practice, whereas most of them were speaking from theory. They could not say that I was wrong. What I was telling them was fact – they had just never experienced any of it themselves. Eventually, some agreed to accept my statements.

I wrote a pamphlet called *The Care and Cleaning of Leather and Latex*. So many people neglect this most important aspect. Greater care must be taken of latex, because of its fragility. But don't forget to oil your leather! It is so disappointing to hug someone in a leather jacket and feel an almost cardboard-type substance, rather than the great feel of leather that has been well-tended. The difference is like day and night, especially to a leatherman. So many people come up to me and say, "You sold me my first jacket, my first pair of boots, my first pair of chaps and I still have them, and they are my favorite pieces of clothing…" That's really great. And I always showed them how to take care of their leather, which they never forgot, you know. People tell me, "I put neatsfoot oil on my jacket just like you showed me, and I've still got it – and you were right, it's really kept its suppleness." I'm very happy to hear that. People were always asking me what was best to use, so I thought a pamphlet would be a useful addition to their reference libraries. I sold three hundred and fifty copies and considered this reasonable. It was quite short and to the point.

In 1989 I finally went to another Imperial Court coronation. I was most honored to walk up the runway with Ruth Brinker, the wonderful lady who started Project Open Hand. We both received The Baroness Von Dieckoff Humanitarian Award. I was absolutely thrilled and delighted for both Ruth and myself. In 1990 I went up again with Allison Moet, head nurse on the AIDS Ward at San Francisco General Hospital, where I have now worked as a volunteer for sixteen years. We were received as Man and Woman of the Year. This was a wonderful thrill and a total surprise.

They say that things come in threes. That happened to me. 1989-1990 was a bad year. First, there was the Loma Prieta earthquake. I was in a supermarket looking for a bottle of sherry. I was just reaching for it when all hell broke loose. All the lights went out, the floor started shaking and bottles were flying through the air! I could not see anything. It was a miracle that I was not cut, but I was covered in every kind of alcohol from head to foot. The manager of the store came out and saw the mess. Piles of cereals had tipped up all over the floor, blocking the aisle. It was a very frightening experience, not knowing what would happen and not being able to move!

Then I went to Provincetown on vacation. The day after I arrived, there was a warning announcing the arrival of "Hurricane Bob." It was terrible. There was no power for three days, all the restaurants were closed, all there was to eat was sandwiches and you could not leave, as the airport was closed. I have never been back there. It was the most disappointing travel experience of my life.

Thirdly, at 7:45 on a Saturday morning, while I was living on Folsom Street, the building next door to me caught fire. We don't know for sure, but we think we know what started it. There was a little apartment building to the left of what was then The Ramrod and is now My Place. We think there were two boys smoking in bed who were somewhat stoned, although they denied it. It was a wooden building, and the fire spread quickly. The Ramrod was closed for several months. The fire burned the entire roof off the bar. I was on the third floor, and the fire came in over the roof. It was funny in a way. I had a roommate and also a houseguest from England. We had three bedrooms and we all had tricks. I had been fast asleep. The firemen came spilling in through the roof with their hoses, ruining all my carpets and furniture with water. The boy in the front room had a dick in him and I banged on the door and said, "There's a fire! You have to get up. The fire department is coming." He said, "I've got a dick up my butt; it feels so good I don't want to move!" I said, "Well, I'm sorry, you're going to have to!" Roger, my houseguest from England, was leaving the next day and the fire department threw his airline ticket out the window. My poor house guest! They burst into his room, throwing all kinds of things out of the window to try to stop the fire from spreading. This included his short-wave radio, his expensive watch and his return ticket to London! He was going by British Overseas Airways and it was the middle of the night and we could not get hold of them to try and get a new ticket issued. He was due to leave the next day. We did manage eventually to get a new ticket. It was just in time, as we had to wait until their offices in London opened. It was the only time I've ever been in an ambulance: I got smoke inhalation. I got my trick out of bed, and we were running around trying to get our clothes on and get the people in the front room to stop playing. I also knocked on my roommate's door. He said that he too was having sex! I told him there was a fire and there would soon be firemen in his bedroom and they would not want to join in. Eventually he grudgingly said, "OK. I'll come out."

I had just put in a brand new kitchen with a no-wax floor, a butcher block cupboard, a dishwasher and new kitchen cabinets. I had to leave all that behind. I had no renter's insurance. It was going to take them six months to repair the damage. I could not wait, so two friends helped out, putting me up on their sofa beds for three months until I found a suitable new place to live and moved. It was difficult doing this and working at the same time. I owe a deep debt of gratitude to the friends who took me in. I met one guy at the Watering Hole who put me up for two or three weeks, and then his roommate came back from Portland and I had to move. And so my very good friend Arthur put me up and I stayed on his sofa bed until I found a place. I found a very nice flat on 18th and Eureka, which was great, just beautiful. I was there for a couple of years before I met Johnie. I really did not want to leave that flat but had no option. It was a three-bedroom, with large rooms, for $700 a month. Also, it was just a block away from the original Mr. S store on 7th Street between Folsom and Howard.

I lost the first Mr. S catalog in that fire. I lost a lot of my personal stuff, which was irreplaceable and that was very sad, considering the fire didn't even start in our building. There are three catalogs that I produced that I don't have at all. I lost almost everything. My landlord was able to recompense me for the wall-to-wall carpeting, which was over $2000, but I lost nearly all my furniture. I didn't lose any clothes, fortunately, but I lost a lot of pictures, photographs, papers and memorabilia that were irreplaceable, so that was bad. I also lost a wonderful flat in a great area at a very good rent. It had big rooms, a huge kitchen and a huge bathroom. It was really great and it was a great shame. But I'd have had to move anyway eventually, because there were a lot of stairs and my lungs are not good with stairs. That is why we moved from the last place before I came here, because the stairs were so bad and Johnie had neuropathy.

At one time I had a lot of problems with people trying to break into the store, usually by breaking the glass in the window. It was so annoying; the alarm would almost always go off around 3 a.m. The cops would get there pretty fast. Once there was a burglar hiding under a table with three leather jackets on him. A police dog sniffed him out and he was arrested. It was quite an expense getting a new window put in, and also the alarm wiring had to be replaced. I was not covered by insurance for this, either. I had had no experience in anything like this and never thought to do it. I certainly wish that I had insured against fire. I would like to say that, contrary to popular belief, you do not make a fortune out of the leather business. You have to employ good craftsmen to make the clothing and they get good salaries. Also, there is an unavoidable waste of leather and those skins are expensive. Plus, you have to finance a large stock. Somehow we always managed to cover payroll for the staff, even when things were tight. I often did not take any salary at all myself. When things got better, I compensated for that when it was possible.

I remember another big fire on Folsom Street, when an entire block burned down. There had been a stock warehouse for Rush poppers on that block, and it was thought that this was the cause of the fire, although this was never confirmed. The papers were full of the news. Diane Feinstein, who was by then the mayor, was shown standing in a charred playroom. The fire chief said that he feared there might have been slaves chained to beds! It caused quite a stir all over town.

CHAPTER 5

Life after Mr. S

In 1989 I had the chance to sell Mr. S and did so. I had run it for twenty years, and whilst I loved dealing with the public, I had contracted emphysema and it was hard to work at the pace that I had been maintaining. I stayed on to help with the transfer until March 1990, then I bade farewell to the staff. I used to go in during Leather Week in the succeeding years, as it was such a busy time and many of my old friends and customers from way back came into the store. I did this for a few years and always enjoyed it. I decided to try to start a new company after I left Mr. S and thought that it should be something that was S/m oriented. I called it The Supply Master. Great name, I thought. The idea was to offer items not made from leather which could be sold to people who wanted to play, but who could not afford expensive leather toys. I had restraints, slings, etc., made from car seat belting material, and some novel ideas, but regretfully it did not go over. After struggling with it for two years, I closed it down and finally retired completely, except for volunteer work.

When it was fun and exciting, it was great. When it was a hassle and not fun, it was not so great. The emphysema had a lot to do with my decision. I couldn't lift anything. I couldn't do stairs. I couldn't walk long distances. I'd run out of breath and it got increasingly difficult. I couldn't work the long hours. I tried to do so many different things, but there was a limit to what I really could do. I wasn't getting any younger either, so I felt it was time. I was just glad that the business was able to carry on and that most of the staff I had started with were still there. Now, of course, it's a giant mushroom. Who would have known that it would have gotten as big as it is now! That is due to Richard Hunter, the current owner of Mr. S, who has done such a wonderful job preserving and maintaining the high standard of quality and service that I always strived to uphold.

Just before Thanksgiving in 1992, I walked out on to the patio of The Lone Star and there stood Johnie Garcia. He was looking lonely and at the same time so desirable. Our eyes met and it was love at first sight. He took me to his home, which was an apartment on State Street on the fourth floor with no elevator. It was tough getting to the top of the stairs with emphysema, but I did not care, even though I was breathless when I got there. He was such a wonderful person and was always such a pleasure to be with. We had a great deal in common. I really felt that our union was meant to be and we needed each other, in different ways. After the first visit, I returned regularly. He often used to have dinner waiting for me when I got back after working on the AIDS ward. He was always a joy to me. Even when he got sick, he never complained and was always good company. We would often just sit together, watch a movie on TV and hold hands, totally content. The stairs became too much for both of us, so we found a very nice flat together on Potrero Hill. It was very nice with a sweet Japanese landlady. It had a wonderful bathroom with a Jacuzzi in the tub. It was the nicest flat I had ever lived in, and very modern.

Johnie brought so much joy into my life, more than I had ever known before, and I miss him a lot. He really depended on me for so much, and I really enjoyed being Daddy and being needed. It gave an extra quality to my life. It was really tough having to move in 1995. It was two weeks after Johnie passed away and I moved into the new apartment that we had intended to move into together. He had worked out where each piece of furniture would go and I arranged the new place just as he had wanted it to be. His family was like extended family to me. Had it not been for his sister, I would have had great difficulty getting through the funeral. I was very saddened to hear that she recently had a heart attack and died. She was only in her mid-forties. She was indeed a very wonderful woman and I miss her a lot. We used to e-mail each other regularly. She met a man on the Internet. He flew to San Francisco to meet her and she fell in love with him.

They drove back to his home in Missouri and lived happily together. I was so happy for her. If anyone deserved happiness, she certainly did.

In 1996, on the first anniversary of the opening of Daddy's bar on Castro Street, Daddy Philip Turner honored me with the title "Daddy of the Year." I have always done what I could to support him when he needed it and he has always been a very special friend to me. I admire him tremendously for all the hard work he does for the community. He has such a big heart and does everything with such style and efficiency. If anyone has lived up to the title "Daddy," it is Philip Turner, a truly great man. I would also like to take my hat off to Daddy Don Thompson. After doing benefits pretty well on my own for ten years, Don took over all my events and lifted a huge burden from my shoulders.

I am sure that most people do not realize the tremendous amount of work involved in producing a benefit. There are so many things to do and remember. If it is a contest, you need to select good judges, choose the right venue, book the date, get out press releases, make contestant application forms, make the score sheets, arrange for entertainers and get at least fourteen or fifteen volunteers, especially if there is to be a raffle and auction. These are always good money-makers. I used to work almost exclusively for AEF. As they got bigger and more people were doing benefits for them, I expanded a bit.

I was invited to join the steering committee of The Leathermen's Discussion Group. We meet monthly to decide on future topics and have been donated a room at Eros. We ask participants to make a small donation, which is given to an AIDS charity. We have a huge variety of topics and practical demonstrations, which are interesting, informative and often exciting. I particularly enjoyed the branding demo, which was beautifully and sensitively presented. I also enjoyed tremendously the talk and demonstration on S/m hypnotism, presented by the great and most regrettably late, Hal Heller. What a wonderful man, admired by so many; he is very much missed in the leather community.

One really exciting event that happened in San Francisco was a seminar for one hundred and fifty gay and lesbian future leaders who came to learn about every aspect of gay life. It was an educational smorgasbord for young people. They were from cities all over the States, mostly in their late teens and early twenties. These were the youth who were chairing the gay pride committees and starting organizations. Every gay community needs leaders of all types – whether they're into or out of leather – and the more experience they can get in every aspect helps them, you see. I was invited to form a panel of experts on all aspects of S/m. There were six of us on that track, all very experienced in our own fields. Joseph Bean was still living here at the time, and he participated. I was so pleased with the quality of the men and women on the panel, which included authors, magazine editors, masters and mistresses, and, of course, myself. After each of us gave a few minutes' talk, we answered some really excellent questions. At the end we got a standing ovation, and we were told that it was the best event of the entire seminar. One boy came up to me afterwards and told me that he had a lover back in Ohio who wanted to experience bondage. The top-boy had no experience but really wanted to please his partner. This boy was really good-looking and also very nice. Being the painfully shy person that I am, I said to him, "Well, if you would be willing to change roles for one night, it would be my pleasure to tie you up and explain what I am doing so you will know what to do when you get back home." He said "fine" and it sure was! Woof! What a hot experience.

I did fund-raisers for other charities, like the Godfather Service Fund, which was started by Tony Travisso. They serviced twelve hospitals in the Bay Area, giving AIDS patients robes, slippers, toiletries and teddy bears, which are so much appreciated by new patients coming onto the AIDS wards. Due to the cocktail medications, fewer AIDS patients are in the hospitals these days, so the Godfathers decided to close down their operation, but the pleasure they brought to hundreds of AIDS patients can never be overstated. I also raised funds for Sojourn, the volunteer chaplains at S.F. General Hospital who give comfort to the bereaved and support to patients with AIDS. I returned to work at General Hospital after two years at Davies, and though at one time there were twenty-four volunteers, we are now down to two. I do get to train new volunteers as they are found. However, they rarely seem to stay. Burnout was and is a major problem amongst volunteers. It is important that the nurses get all the help they can. Staff numbers have been cut and they really appreciate the help I am able to give them.

We are in the sixteenth year of the San Francisco Leather Daddy/Daddy's boy contests and it is so great to have a committee of daddies to help produce benefits. We split things that have to be dealt with between us. We are each responsible for contributing a factor towards the success of the event. I did it on my own for ten years, and it is indeed a lot of work. There are so many details that have to be remembered. Eventually we developed a group of daddies who work together in unison to produce events, and that took a tremendous lot off my plate. The daddies have become serious leaders and role models in the community, which pleases me a lot. They are a wonderful group of men to work with. I still enjoy helping with benefits, and it's amazing that this continues on and still raises badly-needed funds for AIDS charities year after year. The demand does not stop. AEF is a volunteer-based organization and ninety-five cents of every dollar collected goes back to the community. That is why they get so much support from everyone. Because the fund was started by leathermen and since there is always leather representation on the board of directors, the leather community feels justly proud of AEF's achievements.

I miss some of the leather bars of the past that were so different from what we know today. I especially liked The Ambush. Everyone was there to have a good time, and there was no posing or attitudes. It was on three floors, with a big bar on the ground floor level. Upstairs was a cafeteria with great food, and people used to play bridge up there. On the top floor was a good leather shop with a nice variety of items for sale. Febe's, on the corner of 11th & Folsom, was on two levels with a fair-sized bar downstairs, and Nicodemus of A Taste of Leather had a leather shop upstairs, in addition to his big store down the road on Folsom near 6th Street. Other bars I enjoyed were The Black and Blue, Folsom Prison, The Hungry Hole Saloon, The Red Star Saloon, the original Watering Hole and The Brig, where I had a night store before opening at The Eagle. The Ramrod had great Sunday afternoon movies and The Cave was right across the road from the Mr. S store. It had strong S/m overtones and was definitely a leatherman's bar. I always used to enjoy Sunday brunch in San Francisco. The place to go used to be Lenny Mollet's Chez Mollet or 527 Club on Bryant Street. We used to eat out on the patio, and it was a big social meeting place. Apart from out-of-town visitors, I would know almost everyone in the place and made many lasting friends there.

There has been a remarkable change in the bars on Folsom Street. Many disappeared. Others have been through several changes of name and, in some cases, format also. From 11th Street downwards, Chaps became a straight bar, The DNA Lounge. Febe's became a straight bar, The Paradise Lounge. The Covered Wagon went through several changes, including being The Drummer Key Club, The Plunge and The Oasis. It is now a straight bar, but it does not seem to be named. The No Name became The Bolt, then The Brig and is now The Powerhouse. The Ramrod became Folsom New World and is now called My Place. Several bars have closed down altogether, and some new ones have opened. The Hole in the Wall is owned by the same management as The Eagle Tavern, which was originally just called The Eagle. The Loading Dock is on Mission Street and Mr. S Leather opened a night store there, after the one at The Eagle Tavern closed. On Castro Street, Daddy's has really helped to bring leather back to the neighborhood and the venue is active in AIDS fundraising. There are some fun new fundraising events at Daddy's including Buttrageous. The Edge hosts The Basket Contest. They both bring in a good crowd and raise money for good charities. *The Bare Chest Calendar* seems to be carrying on a great tradition and the quality of contestants is very high. This has truly been a wonderful event that has always been done to benefit AEF, which is still my favorite charity. I would like to mention Danny Williams, who is a comedian and who just never says no when he is asked to do a benefit. I have been doing events with him for years and I am so pleased that he is doing so well professionally. He richly deserves all the recognition that he receives.

There are so many good friends that have passed on, who were so much a part of my life here, that I would like to mention a few of them. Gerry Valaire did a lot of work for the community, and I worked with him on many events. His father lived in New Orleans and made gay pride ribbons, and Gerry appointed me as his sales representative. This was after I had left Mr. S. The Pride Parade Committee decided that these ribbons would make perfect armbands for the parade monitors and I got a huge order from them. I was pleased to see the ribbon being worn by so many people in the parade. I sold it to gay stores all over the place. It was perfect for giftwrapping, costume making and many other uses.

Michael Valerio orchestrated The Folsom Street Fair. I lived at 8th and Folsom and would wake up on the Sunday morning of the fair at 6 a.m. to the sounds of him setting up the booths. I made coffee for any of his volunteers who wanted it.

Patrick Toner, IML 1985, was a good friend and a wonderful man – a real inspiration to the community. He started the Up your Alley block party and fair, which was always very successful. He co-emceed for me with another good friend, Christian Heron, who was San Francisco Leather Daddy II and the original Marlboro Man. He ran The Wedge Program for the Mayor's office, which deals with AIDS education for young people. They had great chemistry together. Patrick and I also judged contests together and always had a lot of fun doing it. He endeared himself to everyone he met.

I will never forget the very wonderful Rita Rockett, who fortunately is still very much with us and who has served food to the patients on the AIDS ward at San Francisco General Hospital for many years. She sat with Patrick on a panel judging leather daddies. They had so much fun doing it together, and Rita was amazing. I wondered how as a straight, though most understanding, woman did she know to ask some of the great questions that she asked.

Terry Thompson managed The Eagle and did so much to help with AIDS fundraisers. He always invited me to the employee Christmas party, which I always enjoyed. There are more – too numerous to mention – but they will never be forgotten, and I miss them all every day of my life. Mention has already been made of my three greatest friends: Zach Long, George Burgess and Hank Cook. The work that we did together for the AEF was a very important part of my life; we spoke on the phone at least once a day, sometimes twice. Their passing has left a void, and I can never replace them. Of the sixteen San Francisco Leather Daddies, seven have passed away – all wonderful men. They all worked hard for the community and will not be forgotten, and I am pleased that their names are on the trophy that stands in the back bar of The Eagle.

I used to enjoy the Living in Leather conferences that were held in Seattle or Portland. It was a great get-together of the leather community and helped form closer bonds between the men and women. They always had the most interesting workshops. I was frequently invited to do one on The Care and Cleaning of Leather and Rubber and always got some interesting questions. People had no idea how to take care of their leather. That's how I ended up writing the pamphlet that I did. I was regularly asked to do that seminar for people, and we always had a pretty good crowd. Sometimes I would talk about my experiences along the way and some of the stories and the funny things that happened.

In 1999 I received The Pantheon of Leather Forebear Award in New Orleans. I am in great company with this award. So many great people have won it in the past, including Tom of Finland, who I knew for many years until his untimely death from lung cancer. We were both associate members of The 69 Club of the United Kingdom, which was the first club I ever joined when I came out into leather in 1969. Those were early days in the leather community. I learned a lot very quickly from my fellow club members, which helped me in later years to pass on advice to novices who often came to me with questions. I am happy to say that I still do that to this very day.

In 2000 I had my greatest thrill. I received a phone call from my friend Graylin Thornton, who was International Mr. Drummer 1993, inviting me to a meeting of The GLBT Historical Society as his chaperone. His lover was out of town, and I was supposed to see that he behaved! I soon learned that it was a ruse to get me there, and I discovered that they had named a fund to benefit The Leather Archives and Museum in Chicago: *The Selby Fund*. I had no idea; it was the best-kept secret in San Francisco! They produced a pin with my profile on it, with *LA&M* and *The Selby Fund* on it. Big thanks go to Joe Gallagher and Graylin Thornton for giving me this great honor. Normally this kind of thing is awarded posthumously. They also gave me a wonderful trophy, which is now being engraved. It is something to remind me always of this wonderful event, which took place – by his gracious permission – in the home of Richard Hunter. So many charities, especially those looking after people with AIDS, need our help and support. It is truly wonderful that we are able to continue doing this, year after year, and are still able to help finance the work of the museum. The amount already raised is phenomenal and a tribute to the strength, love, generosity and dedication of the leather community. You are my family. I love and appreciate you all, more than words can fully convey.

In 2001 I was invited to ride in the Gay Pride Parade behind the wonderful Mama Sandy Reinhardt, who was one of the Grand Marshals that year. She took over the big Leather Walk fundraiser for AEF. She increased the amount raised by a huge amount and also increased the number of people actually participating in the walk. She started the Breast Cancer Emergency Fund dinner, which also has helped raise badly-needed funds. She has adopted over three hundred and twenty-five boys from within the leather community, many of whom are more than willing to help her in her fundraising endeavors. She rode in the parade like a goddess, in a chariot pulled by a leather man wearing a wonderful leather carnival mask and leather wings. She was followed by two boys in a cage, whose bodies had been painted with stripes to make them look like tigers. I was in a car behind them, and there was also a huge contingent of motorbikes and leather men marching. It was most impressive, and we got a huge welcoming reception from the crowd lining Market Street as we passed by. It was a glorious sunny San Francisco day.

In San Francisco there is an award ceremony that must be unique in the world. One could say, "only in San Francisco" would they give awards for sexual prowess. They are known as The Golden Dildeaux Awards. Of course, they are not serious awards, but one can vote for one's friends in the community at a dollar per vote, and the money goes to AEF. The award is wooden and in the form of a golden painted penis. I was nominated and won The Golden Arm Award for fisting. I was really surprised to win this, but also very pleased.

AEF held a Gala in place of their usual annual dinner. It was at The Herbst Theater, with *hors d'oeuvres*, a great variety show and an awards ceremony. There I was honored with an Outstanding Contribution Award and was given a wonderful reception from the audience. I was on the silent auction committee and fortunately was very successful in bringing in many of the items for this event.

2002 is a year I will never forget. I was nominated for Grand Marshal of the Gay Pride Parade, which is a great honor. Whilst I did not win, I was the first ever Leather Marshal and was driven in a white convertible with the words "Daddy Alan Selby, Leather Marshal" on flexible magnetic plates on both sides of the car. It was so uplifting to hear shouts of "Daddy Alan!" from both sides of Market Street as we drove down. I had four hot leather boys as wheel monitors, and they added to my pleasure as I happily waved to the crowd along the way. I have been so honored over the past years, and it feels so wonderful to be appreciated for my efforts and thanked for my successes. At the end of the parade I was taken to City Hall for a fabulous reception given by the San Francisco Pride board and was honored with an award from the board for outstanding service to the LGBT community. I met and was photographed with Sir Ian McKellen, Celebrity Grand Marshal, and Armistead Maupin, the author of *Tales of the City*. What an end to a perfect day!

APPENDIX:

San Francisco Leather Daddies/
San Francisco Leather Daddy's boys

San Francisco Leather Daddies

1983   Michael Blair, I (d)

1984   Christian Heran, II (d)

1985   Tom Roller, III (d)

1986   Tom Rodgers, IV

1987   Zach Long, V (d)

1988   Jason Ladd, VI

1989   Jay Smith, VII (d)

1990   Don Thompson, VIII

1991   Joe Scibetta, IX

1992   Irwin Kane, X (d)

1993   Philip Turner, XI (d)

1994   Steve Gaynes, XII

1995   Cornelius Conboy, XIII

1996   Loren Berthelsen, XIV

1997   Patrick Batt, XV

1998   Kelly Showers, XVI (d)

1999   André English, XVII

2000   Keith Truitt, XVIII

2001   Robert Davolt, XIX (d)

2002   Tony Koester, XX

2003   Peter Fiske, XXI

2004   Doug Mezzacapo, XXII

2005   Richard Sprott, XXIII

2006   Warren Williams, XXIV

2007   Glen Tanking, XXV

2008   Ray Middling, XXVI

2009   Gauge Strongarm. XXVII

2010   David S. Meyer, XXVIII

2013   Brett Brockschmidt, XXIX

San Francisco Leather Daddy's boys

1983   Jake Banks, I

1984   Dean Gibson, II

1985   Steve Kajikawa, III

1986   James Buhler, IV

1987   John Cassase, V

1988   Rick Ramiriz, VI

1989   Grant Mickens, VII

1990   Mark Sponseller, VIII

1991   Eric Passler, IX

1992   Bill White, X

1993   Craig Neely, XI

1994   Jim Gibson, XII

1995   Steve Crouse, XIII

1996   Joey Faria, XIV

1997   David Meyer, XV

1998   Todd Kepus, XVI

1999   Lance Brittain, XVII

2000   Bob Dern, XVIII

2001   Brian Stevens, XIX

2002   Will Brunner, XX

2003   Joey Sequeria, XXI

2004   Jorge Vieto Jr., XXII

2005   Phil Lindo, XXIII

2006   Dirk Burns, XXIV

2007   Angle Dunkelberger, XXV

2008   Carl Anderson, XXVI

2009   Mikey Shirts, XXVII

2010   Adam Schwenk, XXVIII

2013   Erik Burkett, XXIX

INDEX

NOTE: "AS" refers to Alan Selby. Page numbers in *italics* indicate photographs.

B

N

U

V

W

Y

CPSIA information can be obtained
at www.ICGtesting.com
Printed in the USA
BVOW08s1349070717

488543BV00002B/149/P